Managing the Learning Process

Philip Waterhouse

McGRAW-HILL Book Company (UK) Limited

London · New York · St Louis · San Francisco · Auckland · Bogotá · Guatemala
Hamburg · Johannesburg · Lisbon · Madrid · Mexico · Montreal · New Delhi
Panama · Paris · San Juan · São Paulo · Singapore · Sydney · Tokyo · Toronto

Published by

McGRAW-HILL Book Company (UK) Limited
MAIDENHEAD · BERKSHIRE · ENGLAND

British Library Cataloguing in Publication Data

Waterhouse, Philip
   Managing the learning process.—(McGraw-Hill
series for teachers)
   1. Teaching
   I. Title
   371.1′02   LB1025.2

   ISBN 0–07–084136–5

Library of Congress Cataloging in Publication Data

Waterhouse, Philip.
   Managing the learning process.
   (McGraw-Hill series for teachers)
   Bibliography: p.
   Includes index.
   1. Classroom management.   I. Title.   II. Series.
   LB3013.W37 1983   371.1′02   82–9983

   ISBN 0–07–084136–5   AACR2

12345 LT 86543

Printed and bound in Great Britain by
Latimer Trend & Company Ltd, Plymouth

Contents

Preface

In 1974 I resigned my headship of a Bristol comprehensive school in order to establish the Resources for Learning Development Unit. This was a four-year experiment continuing the work of the Nuffield Foundation's Resources for Learning Project which had pioneered resource-based learning in the UK.The brief of the new unit was to encourage a shift towards more independent styles of learning in secondary schools. Our strategy was to establish a teachers' cooperative to produce the kind of resources needed for independent learning, and to support experimental classroom work with advice and in-service training.

Producing resources proved to be easy; but bringing about changes in classroom practice was not. Our early experiments in classroom management were disappointing, and sometimes chaotic. A colleague and I set up a 'demonstration classroom', which turned out to be a traumatic experience, forcing us to recognize the gap between ambition and capability, between theory and practice.

We humbly set about the task of trying to improve our own classroom work by careful planning, meticulous preparation, and by analysis of our teaching through observation and deliberation. The eventual outcome was a *system* of classroom management which was designed to support class teaching and small-group work, as well as individual work, with emphasis on the use of a wide repertoire of methods and media within the framework of the whole system.

This book describes the system and shows how it can be used as the basis for regular improvement in teaching. Throughout it emphasizes the collaborative approach, although much can be accomplished by a teacher working alone. It is based on experience with secondary school pupils in the 11 to 16 age range, but primary school teachers will recognize the relevance of the principles and techniques for their own situation.

The book is intended as a practical handbook. The illustrations and checklists could be instantly usable by many teachers, or at least they could serve as models.

In many chapters I have offered firm opinion and advice in preference to seeking shelter under vague and permissive generalizations. As I see it, I must have the courage of my convictions, but I hope that no impression of dogmatism has been given, especially where there are points which could clearly admit a different opinion.

It is hoped that the book may be found useful in the initial training of teachers, and in programmes of in-service education. I should also particularly like to see it brought into service in school-based staff development programmes.

Acknowledgements

I am grateful for permission to include copyright material from the following: Denham, C. and A. Luberman (eds), *Time to Learn*, National Institute of Education. Washington, 1980, pp. 20 and 21; Flanders, N., *Analysing Teaching Behaviour*, Addison-Wesley, Reading, Massachusetts, 1970, p. 34; Galton, M., B. Simon and P. Croll, *Inside the Primary School Classroom*, Routledge and Kegan Paul, London, pp. 12, 13 and 17; Lao Tzu: *Tao Te Ching* (Trans. D. C. Lan), Penguin Classics, Penguin, Harmondsworth, 1963, poem XVII, p. 73; Figure 5.3 is based on a drawing by Shyam Varma (County of Avon, R.L.D.U.).

I should like to express my personal gratitude to: many colleagues in the County of Avon Education service; Richard Stroud (Headmaster), Ray Everett (Head of Humanities), Humanities staff and pupils of Speedwell School, Bristol; Roger Alston (Deputy Head, Nailsea School, Bristol, and formerly Assistant Director of R.L.D.U.) who collaborated with me in our 'demonstration classroom'; the staff of R.L.D.U.; Roger Alston and Arthur Knott (Weston-Super-Mare Teachers' Centre) who read the manuscript and made helpful suggestions; and my wife who typed it, and improved it, and forebore it.

Philip Waterhouse

Part One Introduction

An advance view of teaching and learning

The nature of the problem

Teaching and learning are the concern of a whole education service. As well as teachers there are the politicians, the administrators, the university and college tutors, the advisers and inspectors, the librarians and teachers' centre wardens. All play important roles. But this book concentrates on the improvement of teaching and learning which can be brought about by the cooperative efforts of a team of competent and purposeful teachers. A team of such teachers might be a secondary school department, or an interdisciplinary team, or a year team in a primary or middle school.

Teaching is not as easy as it used to be. There are more pressures in today's society, and greater ambitions and more sophistication within the profession itself. There is much debate about education, conducted publicly and often ferociously with arguments frequently polarized: 'progressive' versus 'traditional'; 'discipline' versus 'freedom'; 'choice' versus 'prescription'. Most sensible teachers do not identify with any one 'movement' but prefer to identify with the children they teach rather than with a set of abstract ideas. They want to strike a decent balance: to use a wide repertoire of methods and styles; to give their pupils a broad experience of different ways of working and learning.

The teacher who wants to improve the quality of classroom life must acquire a great sensitivity to the situations and needs of the pupils, but at the same time adopt a systematic approach to the planning and preparation of classroom work. This is what makes teaching so demanding. On the one hand, it has to be intensely personal and adaptive; on the other hand, it has to be disciplined and systematic. For these reasons many teachers find it advantageous to adopt collaborative styles of working, in order to get the benefits of corporate planning, the best use of resources, and the sharing of personal experiences and knowledge of the pupils.

Definitions

The improvement of teaching and learning is not a once-and-for-all activity. It is a cyclical activity. There is a thinking and planning phase, followed by an action phase, which is followed in turn by another thinking and planning phase, and so on. The cycle can be applied by the team of teachers to its course planning and resources preparation, and it can also be used by the individual teacher in the improvement of individual lessons. It can serve as a short-term device for immediate improvements or a part of a long-term strategy.

The cycle of improvement is simply a way of thinking, and it should not be allowed to become a rigid programme, or to give rise to an excess of meetings or a proliferation of paperwork. At all times the cycle needs to be adapted to the local and immediate situation.

It is possible, however, to define in broad terms the various stages of the cycle.

Fig. 1.1 *The basic cycle*

Review and evaluation

This is the start of the thinking and planning phase. The teachers look back over the past year and ask themselves questions. What actually happened? Are we satisfied with the pupils' motivation and achievements? Did the pupils seem satisfied? What contributed to our successes? What were the likely causes of our failures?

Studies and investigations

When the evaluation has been completed, dissatisfactions, uncertainties, problems, and opportunities may have come to light. These require study and investigation. Some teachers might conduct a survey to find the needs as perceived by the pupils, or by the local community while others might search for new thinking in curriculum, in methods, or in technology, through visits, attendance at courses, or through reading.

McGRAW-HILL series for Teachers

Consulting Editor:
Peter Taylor
School of Education, Bristol University

Objectives

The planning of the next year's work can now go ahead. Objectives are a simple way of stating what it is hoped to achieve. Naturally, the focus must be on the pupils—their knowledge and understanding, their achievements, their maturity.

Commitment and support

Objectives are not likely to be of much help unless people are committed to them and unless support has been gained for them. The gaining of this commitment and support is an essential task of leadership. The aim should be to get deep and personal involvement from as wide a group as possible, for example, the pupils themselves, their parents, other teachers in the school, the Head and senior staff, local authority officers.

Preparation

Now follows the detailed decision-making and preparation before the actual teaching takes place. Resources have to be acquired, learning activities devised, tests written, record keeping arranged, and the classroom itself needs to be prepared.

Classroom work

This is the final stage of the cycle; it is the culmination of all the planning and preparation. It will never be far from the teachers' minds during the planning and preparation stages. What will it be like with these children in this school at this point of time? But good classroom work also relies on attitudes and techniques that are immediate, and for which no amount of planning will substitute. This is the 'sharp end' of education: the face-to-face contact between teacher and pupil.

After the classroom work, or course, the cycle starts again. The description above is only a broad introductory outline. The concept of the cycle of improvement will be explored in more detail in later chapters.

The benefits of the cycle

It is a disciplined way of bringing about improvements

The cycle is planned, and deliberate, and systematic, offering a sequence of activities which serves as a reminder and a checklist. It focuses attention on the important issues which are likely to help bring about improvement.

It is a cooperative way of working

It invites all members of a team to share a common programme, to concentrate on the same things at the same time. It becomes intellectually stimulating to the group and has important benefits for interpersonal relations too.

It introduces an element of objectivity into the improvement of teaching

Teaching is such an intensely personal thing that criticism of teaching is a delicate and dangerous business. It is only when teachers have personally chosen objectives and gained the support of their colleagues that they will feel relaxed in the evaluation of their performance.

It is cumulative

The cycle never ends: the evaluation stage is immediately followed by new thinking and planning for future. Improvements made in one cycle become the base line for improvements in the next.

Part Two The management of the teaching team

1. Planning a teaching programme

The need for planning

Careful and efficient planning is a characteristic of good teaching. This is obvious enough, but the difficulty is that the teacher's day is so crowded with pressures and demands that action can all too easily become merely reflexive. The teacher is barely inside the front door of the school before the first problem presents itself, and he may frequently leave at the end of the day with a feeling of having initiated nothing.

But planning is vital to success: it helps focus the mind on big issues and important considerations; it gives a sense of direction; and it demonstrates the interdependence of different activities and different people. So adequate time must be found for it. It is wrong that teachers should have to fit in planning when and where they can, for example, in lunch hours and after school. Good planning demands time, uninterrupted by the pressures of the moment, and arranged in generous blocks, so that reflective and creative thinking can take place. It is all a matter of priorities, and one of the first actions of the team of teachers who wish to improve their teaching must be to create more time for planning.

Five essential planning questions

Let us suppose that a team of teachers is about to plan a whole year's programme for a particular group of pupils. The team must consider not only the needs of the pupils as they, the teachers, perceive them, but also the demands which society as a whole is legitimately making on the teaching profession. These needs and demands can be examined by asking five essential questions.

1. *What are the basic facts about these pupils, in this school, at this time, which have a bearing on the work now being planned?* What ought we to know about the pupils themselves? What ought we to know about the environment in which they are growing up?
2. *What are the educational objectives for the proposed programme?* In other words, what are our ambitions for our pupils? What new understanding and new skills are we hoping to develop in them? What difference are we hoping to make to their thinking and attitudes?
3. *What subject content is to be covered by the programme?* Is it relevant,

up-to-date, useful, stimulating? Is it appropriate to the pupils' general intelligence and intellectual maturity, and will it interest them?

4. *What learning activities must we plan to achieve our objectives and to cover the chosen content?* What will the pupils actually do?

5. *What arrangements will there be for the evaluation of the programme?* How shall we know if our pupils have benefited in the ways that we intended?

This chapter suggests ways of working out the answers to these questions.

What are the basic facts about these pupils in this school which have a bearing on the work now being planned?

It is important to be as systematic as possible in the collection of data. A useful aid is a checklist of questions, which should be devised by the teaching team and subjected to constant review. A ready-made one, which can serve as a starter, is shown in Table 1.1.

Table 1.1 *Basic facts questionnaire*

PLANNING DOCUMENT 1

The pupils themselves

- What is the size of the teaching groups?
- What is the range of their general intelligence (VRQ)?
- How many of them have a reading age of less than 9?
- How do their basic skills match up to the likely requirements of the programme?
- What knowledge do they already have which is relevant to the proposed programme?
- Are they likely to have sufficient intellectual maturity to tackle the proposed programme?
- What kind of 'personality' does the group as a whole exhibit?
- Do any of the pupils need special care, through maladjustment, deprivation, or social inadequacy?
- Do any of the pupils need special care on account of exceptionally high ability or special giftedness?

The pupils' environment

- How does the proposed programme relate to the whole curriculum for the year-group in question?
- How does the proposed programme relate to the whole school course in the subject?
- What contribution will the programme make to the whole curriculum policies of the school?
- How does the proposed programme relate to existing LEA policies and services?
- What resources (people and money) are likely to be available?

Of course, the answers cannot be precise at the outset. The real value of a checklist like this is to serve as a constant reminder during the whole of the planning stage. So frequent reference back is desirable.

What are the educational objectives for the proposed programme or unit of study?

The educational objectives of a team of teachers should be stated in a policy document which is kept or displayed in a prominent position. The statement will serve as a guide to all planning and preparation, although many programmes will only relate to a selection of the objectives. The important thing is for the team to *use* the statement.

Educational objectives should be thought of as the outcomes, the achievements, or the results that we hope for. So they are usually expressed as the *capabilities* that the pupils will acquire: new knowledge and understanding, new and more sophisticated ways of thinking, new attitudes and values.

The main benefit of thinking about objectives is that it helps guard against the danger of classroom work becoming a mere recital of factual knowledge. Simple knowledge is important, but education should be more than this. It should seek to develop a comprehensive repertoire of intellectual, social and physical skills.

The literature on educational objectives is vast and this is not the place to attempt a critical review of the often conflicting ideas and positions. Instead, a simple scheme is offered, which could be adapted for a wide variety of planning situations. The scheme can be used in two ways: first as a 'map', which reveals the extent of the area to be covered, and shows the relationships between the different objectives; second as a checklist which is used during planning, and can be referred to again and again during detailed preparation. The checklist serves as a reminder; it stops the drift into narrow, fact-dominated teaching. The scheme, shown in Table 1.2, is presented as a classified list of pupil capabilities. The scheme will certainly need to be expanded or modified according to the intellectual maturity of the pupils and according to the subject that is to be taught. But the seven major headings should provide a useful framework for a start, and the subheadings should at least provide examples of the kind of thinking that is useful in developing educational objectives. A team should make reference to a selection of the writings listed in the bibliography.

9

Table 1.2 *Pupil capabilities*

PLANNING DOCUMENT 2

1. *Knowledge and understanding*
   - Knowledge of facts
   - Understanding of concepts
   - Understanding of generalizations

2. *Handling knowledge*
   - Finding information from a variety of sources, using a variety of approaches (primary sources, secondary sources, observation, measurement).
   - Presenting and communicating information and ideas in a variety of ways and through a variety of media.
   - Interpreting graphic and symbolic data, e.g., pictures, charts, graphs, diagrams, maps.

3. *Thinking critically*
   - Recognizing underlying assumptions.
   - Identifying the main ideas or the central issues.
   - Weighing evidence and drawing warranted conclusions.
   - Formulating and testing hypotheses.

4. *Working with other people*
   - Cooperating with others in the pursuit of common ends.
   - Developing empathy.
   - Understanding the role of individuals and groups in human society.

5. *Working with equipment*
   - Developing skills and techniques in handling equipment.
   - Using equipment to find and communicate information and ideas.

6. *Using physical skills*
   - Expressing ideas and feelings through bodily movement.
   - Using physical effort to make or change something.

7. *Developing attitudes and values*
   - Developing a scientific approach to human behaviour and technological problems.
   - Developing a humanitarian outlook on the behaviour and problems of others.
   - Developing a willingness to explore personal attitudes and values.

What content is to be covered by the programme and is it relevant and useful?

This is a critical stage in the planning process. What ought these pupils to know and understand? What is right for *them* in their unique situation? What content will serve to develop the pupils' capabilities which have been adopted as objectives?

The choice of subject matter will be influenced by the answers already given to the first two questions on basic facts and educational objectives. It is likely that thinking about content will force an early reconsideration of these two questions. Planning is like that. It is not so much a step by step process on a continuous line; it is more like an ascending spiral, going over the same territory several times, but with improvement and progress being made all the time.

Ruthless selection has to be the order of the day. There has been such an explosion of knowledge, and the demands on the schools are now so great, some kind of sifting process is needed and this can be best done by establishing a set of criteria for testing the relevance and usefulness of the proposed subject matter. The third planning document, shown in Table 1.3, is a list of questions which will serve such a purpose.

Table 1.3 *Criteria for the selection of content*

PLANNING DOCUMENT 3

1. *How does the proposed content fit with and support (a) the whole curriculum for the year group, and (b) the programme for the subject throughout the school?*
   Gaps and overlaps should be identified. Opportunities for mutual aid between subjects should be exploited. The work of previous stages should be built on, and adequate preparation made for the work of later stages.

2. *Are the facts, ideas, and methods up to date?*
   Busy teachers find it difficult to keep up to date in their subject knowledge. Many teachers would make no claim to be subject specialists. Wherever there is any doubt expert help should be sought. Academics and members of professional, industrial, and commercial organizations are often only too pleased to be invited to help, and nothing but good can come from such cooperation.

3. *Does the proposed content help the pupils to understand the fundamental structure of the subject?*
   There are substantial advantages in directing the pupils' thinking towards the fundamentals of the subject. The subject matter is made comprehensible, and detail is more easily mastered, because there is a framework on which to hang it. Understanding the basic principles of a subject also helps the student to transfer his knowledge and understanding, and to apply it in new situations.

4. *Does the proposed subject matter promote the exercise of the higher intellectual skills?*
   The choice of subject matter must support the objectives already adopted. So it must be more than a simple framework of facts: it must be rich enough to provide opportunities for developing concepts, seeing relationships, making generalizations, and applying knowledge to new situations.

11

5. *Does the proposed subject matter contain knowledge and viewpoints that are in tune with the social and cultural attitudes of the times?*
   What does society as a whole appear to desire in its young people? Are there emphases in knowledge, in intellectual and social skills, which seem to be rated highly in these times?

6. *Does the proposed subject matter strike a good balance between breadth and depth?*
   Breadth gives a good coverage of the subject; depth means a better understanding of important concepts and basic principles. Careful selection can ensure that the pupils get the most out of the subject in the limited time available.

7. *Does the proposed content come within the range of the pupils' general intelligence and intellectual maturity?*
   This brings us back again to our basic facts. There are no hard and fast rules to apply, but the question needs to be asked to prevent any serious mismatch between the demands of the subject matter and the pupils' intelligence and intellectual maturity.

8. *Is the proposed content likely to appeal to the pupils?*
   This seems obvious but it is a dangerous area, and teachers often fall into the trap of justifying what they choose to teach solely on the grounds of pupil interest. But interest can be transitory and idiosyncratic, and it should not be allowed to dominate the selection of content. Instead it should be used as *one* relevant factor.

Again it has to be stated that the questions and criteria need to be modified and adapted to suit individual situations. The eight questions have been only briefly elaborated, but each in turn could become a substantial debate within the team. This is a matter for sensible pragmatism. During one cycle a team may decide to give only the briefest consideration to the question of content, preferring to concentrate on other planning matters. During another cycle the team may decide to debate at length the issues involved in the selection of content. In either case, the existence of a suitable checklist of questions will serve as a quick check or as a starting point for a more extended discussion.

What learning activities seem appropriate for the objectives and content of each unit of study within the programme?

By now, the practical teacher will be asking the question: what are the teacher and pupils actually going to do? Real planning must surely be concerned with *action*.

So this question is all to do with styles, methods, and media, and the busy teacher might reasonably hope to be told which is the 'best buy' from all the available choices. There is really no such thing. In spite of a lot of research, no one has come up with a simple answer as to which is the best way of learning and teaching. In fact, there seems to be very little to differentiate between the effectiveness of the various styles and methods. Common sense and experience suggest the two principles outlined below.

1. Give the pupils a wide experience of different teaching and learning styles. They will learn something about themselves in the process. They will respond favourably to the variety of activities and experiences. And they will stand a better chance of developing in themselves a wide range of intellectual skills.

2. In the use of a variety of teaching and learning styles, it is wrong to make choices in a haphazard way. Choose the most appropriate style for each learning situation. Aim for *planned variety*.

Table 1.4 suggests a number of variables and illustrates the range of possible styles.

Table 1.4 *Examples of variables and their ranges of styles*

Variable	Range of styles
The source of new information and ideas	The teacher . . . . . . learning resources
The source of guidance for learning	The teacher . . . written guidance . . . no guidance (dependent) (semi-independent) (totally independent)
Group size	Large group . . . class . . . small-group . . . pair . . . individual
Method of learning	Reception learning . . . . . . discovery learning

The good teacher will use a wide range of styles, making a deliberate choice for each unique situation. *Sequencing* the activities is an important aspect of the art of teaching. Table 1.5, planning document 4, offers a model of a typical sequence, with brief justifications of the choices of styles, methods, and media. Again, this is only a model to help thinking about the sequence of learning activities. In certain situations, it would be possible to justify sequences that are markedly different. However, this one will work well and will give a wide variety of learning activities in a meaningful and useful sequence.

Table 1.5 *The sequence of learning activities*

PLANNING DOCUMENT 4

1. *The introductory phase* The needs at this stage are:
- to arouse pupils' awareness, imagination, and interest;
- to give pupils an 'advance organizer' of the subject matter, a sort of aerial reconnaissance to create a clear mental picture of the whole;
- to provide the pupils with a framework of the main ideas of the unit of study, a sort of scaffolding to which they can attach the bits of new learning.

The appropriate methods might be:
- vivid, clear, exciting exposition by the teacher;
- class dialogue in order to use the pupils' existing knowledge as a starting point.

Media will play an important part:
- well-prepared OHP transparencies;
- film, filmstrip, TV or radio broadcast.

2. *The development phase* The needs at this stage are:
- to acquire detailed knowledge;
- to gain understanding of concepts;
- to practice skills and the application of principles.

Characteristics of the phase could be:
- individual or paired working;
- use of resources and prepared guidance;
- resources and guidance tailored as closely as possible to individual abilities and needs;
- an emphasis on concentration and on personal responsibility.

3. *The recapitulation phase* The needs at this stage are:
- to make use of the knowledge and understanding gained;
- to report back, to discuss, to share knowledge and experiences, to review, to compare, to cooperate and to compete.

Characteristics of this phase could be:
- small-group working;
- use of games, simulations, problem-solving activities, and group projects;
- an emphasis on the skills of working in groups.

What arrangements will there be for the evaluation of the programme?

This is still a relatively untried concept in teaching. For a long time evaluation studies have been an important component in educational development projects, and, for the most part, have been conducted by trained research workers. Evaluation in schools, however, needs to be different; it *has* to be largely internal and subjective because the time and resources are simply not available to do otherwise. The lack of objectivity can be partly overcome by using a number of different perceptions and a number of different techniques. Planning Document 5, shown in Table 1.6, offers a matrix from which to choose. Cells that seem to offer particularly fruitful approaches are identified by blobs.

Table 1.6 *Checklist of evaluation techniques*

PLANNING DOCUMENT 5

The techniques	The teachers	The pupils	Parents	Visiting colleagues	Advisers and tutors	Head teachers	Local community
Tests		●					
Questionnaires	●	●	●				●
Checklists	●						
Interviews		●		●	●	●	
Observations	●			●	●	●	
Structured discussions	●	●	●	●	●	●	●
Ratings	●				●	●	

Some notes on Table 1.6

People The teachers themselves and the pupils will play a leading part in the evaluation. Assistance from other people is bound to be somewhat limited. 'Visiting colleagues', however, is a category which could be exploited to advantage. An example might be the leader of a team doing similar work in a neighbouring school. Such a person's observations would be particularly valuable if presented in the form of a short written report which could form the subject of a team discussion. The arrangement could be reciprocal so that a feeling of mutual support could be built up in the two teams.

Techniques The *tests* given to the pupils at the end of a unit of study will provide valuable data for the evaluation. However, the tests must be carefully designed with the objectives of the study in mind, so that a general picture of the effectiveness of the unit is created, and, similarly, a measure of the different levels of achievement of the pupils.

Questionnaires These have a wide applicability. Perfect questionnaires (with a high degree of validity) are almost impossible to design, but simple quickly produced questionnaires can often be very helpful and provoke much thought and discussions, in spite of their technical imperfections. The important considerations are:

- make clear decisions about what information is required;
- use structured items (fixed choice) as much as possible in order to help later analysis (simple true/false questions are a good example of this);
- use unstructured items (open-ended) in areas where the respondent's ideas are being sought (for example, 'sentence completion' items can produce excellent contributions from pupils);
- try to link the outcome of the questionnaire with a structured discussion, which will develop some of the conclusions that seem to be emerging.

Checklists A checklist is a useful device for starting and structuring a discussion. The team might produce its own checklist of important questions to be asked about every unit of study, or they could use one of the published checklists which are now available (see bibliography).

Interviews These can be private or public (i.e., in the presence of the team), formal or informal, recorded or not. Usually they are used in conjunction with other techniques like questionnaires and observations.

Observations These can be subjective or objective. This important technique is described at length in Chapter 12.

Structual discussions This technique can be used with all interested people. The structuring is important and the outcomes should be clearly recorded.

Ratings These are subjective assessments made on an agreed scale. It is important that the teachers should accept this form of evaluation, and, if they do, they should be responsible for the design and review of its effectiveness as a technique. Although ratings do tend to be unreliable and biased, they can be used to advantage by a confident and stable team.

The outcomes of evaluation will be the raw data and the analysis of it. The *raw data* will be in the form of test results, completed questionnaires, annotated checklists, reports of interviews and observations, minutes of meetings and rating sheets. *The analysis* will consist partly of a statistical analysis and presentation of numerical data, and partly of an agreed statement by the team, based on a consideration of all the evidence available.

Evaluation, done thoroughly, is a formidable task. No team can hope to start from scratch and produce a full and impressive evaluation at the first attempt. The important need is to get started, and then add a little each year, involve more people, use new techniques. Gradually experience and sophistication will increase and the whole exercise will be firmly embedded in the normal thinking and practice of the team.

Summary

1. Planning is vital and time must be found for it.
2. A team's planning needs to be thoroughly integrated with all the other planning in the school, horizontally and vertically.
3. Five essential planning questions need to be asked and five planning documents should result:
   - the basic facts which have a bearing on the study programme;
   - the educational objectives that will serve as a guide and a checklist;
   - the outline of the content;
   - the sequence of the learning activities proposed;
   - the people and techniques to be used in the subsequent evaluation.

2. The preparation of a study unit

Good planning deserves to be followed by thorough preparation. Preparation is also a team job since it is far too big an undertaking to be left to the individual teacher working in isolation and it is so much better when done cooperatively. The time spent will be a good investment because thorough preparation not only makes classroom work easier but also forms a firm base for future improvements.

The planning period for the whole programme has provided the five documents which, for the most part, relate to the whole teaching programme. Preparation can now go ahead, and it can usually be done in smaller units, each of which can be called a unit of study. This is usually a logical division of the subject matter which may last a class for one week, or several weeks, or even a whole term.

The preparation described here is for a wide range of learning activities, including class teaching, individual work, and small-group work, as described in Chapter 1. There are six main jobs to be done.

1. Collect and organize the learning resources.
2. Prepare guidance for the pupils to use during the periods devoted to individual and small-group work.
3. Prepare text and audiovisual materials for the teacher's use during the class teaching periods.
4. Prepare assessment tests.
5. Prepare a master plan for the teacher's use in the classroom which gives instant information about the resources and guidance available.
6. Prepare a teacher's guide for the teacher's personal preparation.

Collecting and organizing the learning resources

The team's planning documents will guide the choice of resources, but there are a number of other principles to be borne in mind. These are set out below as firm statements, with a brief justification for each.

Choose material for its intrinsic value as data or stimulus material

At this stage do not worry about the suitability of the guidance that may be offered to the user, or even the total lack of it. Good resource material is worth having in its own right; good guidance can always be added later.

Prefer resources that are available in small format

This means going for the small topic booklet, the single sheet of data, the single illustration, the short audio-tape or filmstrip. These have the merit of being specific, and so relate directly to the unit's purposes; also they represent an economic use of resources. (Contrast this with the situation where one pupil is working on one page of a 500-page textbook.)

Normally prefer to buy or borrow rather than make resources

Making resources is so time consuming that it can completely dominate the preparation phase. The results are often inadequately researched, poorly conceived, poorly designed, and unattractively reproduced. Use home production only when other sources have failed to produce what is required.

Acquire numbers of resource items according to the needs of the unit

Class sets are sometimes required, but only where an item is likely to be in constant use by the whole class. For the periods of individual and small-group work small sets (5 to 10 copies) are best; and this allows a much larger range of resources to be acquired. Many items will be used only for occasional reference purposes; the single copy is appropriate here. Think of the classroom resources as a small specialist library.

Investigate resource possibilities outside the classroom

The school library/resources centre, other subject departments, the Local Authority support services, may have resources that can be used or borrowed. It is particularly important to consider using the resources of the school library as a natural extension of the work of the classroom. This is an economic way of working and it also provides invaluable learning experiences for the pupils.

As the resources are acquired, the problem of devising a storage and retrieval system has to be faced. Many teams with a long experience in building up resource collections may wish to use sophisticated systems. This needs to be approached with caution; sophisticated systems need to be set up carefully, and they use up the teacher's time in maintenance. Most teams will settle for a very simple system in which each resource item of a unit of study is simply identified by its *accession number*. That is to say, the first resource item to be acquired is number 1, the second is 2, and so on, quite regardless of the subject content of the items. This system is simple for the teacher to set up, and simple for the pupils to use.

Some kind of box system is the best for storage. Library boxes or tray systems work equally well.

The great virtue of the accession number system of classification is that the teacher can go on adding resources throughout the preparation phase, without feeling that the system of classification is getting in the way.

Preparing guidance for individual and small-group learning

There is a lot to be said for having the guidance prepared for pupils kept strictly separate from the resource material. This means that the resource material provides the data and the stimuli, but it does *not* contain instructions, tasks, and questions for the pupil. The main advantage of this arrangement is that it gives great flexibility. A given resource item can serve a wide range of pupils *provided differentiated guidance* is available to them. The same resource item can often provide data for use in a number of quite different topics. Another advantage is that it is much simpler for the teacher to prepare differentiated guidance based on one resource item than to create differentiated resources.

Nevertheless there is a place for structured learning materials which link stimuli and guidance in the one format. Subjects and topics which are sequential and involve practical skills lend themselves well to this treatment.

The aim of prepared guidance is to take the pressure off the teacher during the classroom operations. It is too much to expect that the teacher can devise tasks tailored to individual needs on the spur of the moment and give adequate guidance as well. It is too much to expect that the teacher can repeat the task instructions to each pupil in turn as the need arises.

The prepared guidance usually takes the form of a printed task or job card; or it can be an audio-tape. It is important to stress that the *prepared* guidance is not the only guidance that the pupil will receive. It should be thought of as a starter for discussion. In the hands of a skilful teacher the task card is a flexible tool; it saves time, but it can be modified, extended or contracted according to the needs of the individual pupil and the unique learning situation.

The task card

However adaptable they may be, good task cards are so important to the success of individual and small-group work that time and care spent on them is a sound investment. Ideally the task card ought to do all the following:

- Provide a title for the work to be done.
- Set educational objectives.
- Test previous learning to determine the pupil's readiness for the task.
- Specify the learning resources to be used.
- Instruct the pupil in the tasks to be done, and give guidance about methods and styles.
- Test to determine if the pupil has understood the work and achieved the standard expected.

The two test items, often called the pre-test and the post-test, are only necessary when the learning tasks are sequential and the desired outcomes are capable of being clearly defined and identified.

Using task cards

The two task cards shown in Tables 2.1 and 2.2 on pages 22 and 23 were prepared for a study unit on the Port of Bristol for use in history and geography lessons with pupils in the 11–13 age range.

Resource items   The resource items referred to are:

- *Item 9:* A collection of contemporary accounts of the practices of the slave trade.
- *Item 10:* A booklet entitled *The Anti-Slave Trade Movement in Bristol* published by the Historical Association. Adult and academic, but a rich narrative of the struggles of the abolitionists in Bristol.
- *Item 11:* An audio-tape to help slow readers by providing a helpful commentary on item 9, and some straight readings from it.
- *Item 12:* An audio-tape to help pupils get to grips with item 10.

Objectives   Pupils should be encouraged to write out the objectives: they will benefit from an exposure to the concepts associated with their own thought processes.

Variation in use   The two task cards are clearly differentiated. Number 16 is straightforward and gives plenty of support while number 17 is much more challenging and open-ended. The two cards provide adequate 'starter' material for the guidance of all pupils in a mixed ability class. Each card is capable of infinite variation in the amount of support and guidance given. Able pupils have given a good account of themselves using task card 17 (Table 2.2) without any additional support. But the same card has been used effectively with well-motivated pupils of only average ability by the teacher giving additional help with the structuring of the answer. In just the same way task card 16 can be made accessible to very slow pupils, but could equally be made more challenging for a more able pupil.

Table 2.1 *Port of Bristol task card*

---

16. Bristol and slavery

Objectives: ● to use evidence from contemporary sources;
● to understand the reasons for slavery;
● to sympathize with the plight of the slaves.

You will need: items 9 and 11

Your tasks
1. Listen to the tape. It will help you to understand the events described in the booklet.
2. Make an interesting page under each of the following headings:
   ● Capturing slaves in West Africa
   ● Life on board the slave ships
   ● Life on the plantations

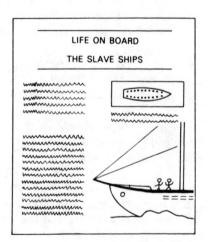

Make the page layout look interesting, as shown in the diagram. You can try other layouts.

Table 2.2   *Port of Bristol task card*

---

17.   Bristol and slavery

Objectives: ● to use evidence from contemporary sources;
● to understand the reasons for slavery;
● to sympathize with the plight of the slaves;
● to analyse the arguments used by the
anti-slave trade movement.

You will need: items 9, 10 and 12

Your tasks
1.   Read the whole of item 9 thoroughly.
2.   Study item 10, using the tape (item 12) to guide you.
3.   Write a letter to an eighteenth century MP urging him to vote for the abolition of the slave trade. You can collect additional evidence in the library. (Look up 'Slavery' in the subject index.) Make sure that your letter would satisfy these tests:
● it must have a lot of *detailed information* about the practices of the trade;
● wherever possible it must quote the *sources of evidence* and give some idea of their reliability;
● it must appeal to the MP's *heart* as well as to his head.

Task card writing

Task card writing is an art which can be developed with practice. It needs to be developed because it is probably the most important single activity of the preparation phase and good task cards are one of the foundation stones of good teaching. A few hints on their preparation will be useful.

1.   Avoid as much as possible the fact extraction–fact reproduction type of task.
2.   Aim to develop higher order intellectual skills: application of knowledge, analysis, problem solving, evaluation.
3.   Allow the pupil as much decision-making as possible.
4.   Aim to develop organizing skills.
5.   Examine the language of the task card critically for ambiguities and confused writing.

6. Make sure that the language of the task card is *well within* the reading competence of the target pupil.
7. Guide the pupil towards an end-product which will be satisfying in itself.
8. Make sure that the end-product of the pupil's work will prove to be self-explanatory when the work is reviewed at a later date.
9. Use models to suggest ways of tackling a task, and to suggest ways of presenting the finished work.
10. Always test a task card before use.
11. Make a note of confusions and difficulties which arise when the card is in use, so that changes can be made.

Task cards are best stored in a card index box with tabbed dividers. Stout cardboard boxes of the right size make a perfectly adequate cheap substitute. A useful size for a task card is A5, or alternatively the old standard index card size, 203×127 mm. It is worth noting that *card* is not really essential, since task cards printed on ordinary bond or duplicating paper seem to have just as long a life.

Preparing the teacher's master plan

The teacher's master plan (Fig.2.1) is simply a summary of all the resources available for the study unit and all the learning activities that have been prepared. It is mainly useful as instant information during classroom operations.

A well-developed master plan might contain:

- A list of all the classroom resources.
- A list of other resources available outside the classroom.
- A list of the prepared learning activities (class lessons and task cards for small-group and individual work) with a brief reminder of the chosen objectives.
- A network to show the alternative routes through the various learning activities.

Plan design

Since the whole plan needs to be seen at a glance it should be kept to a reasonable size. An arrangement of two separate sheets of A4 paper stuck inside a standard manilla folder works very well.

The left-hand page describes the *learning resources*. The collection of classroom resources has already been described and the master plan needs to do no more than list them alongside their reference numbers. More detail is required for the resources that are available outside the

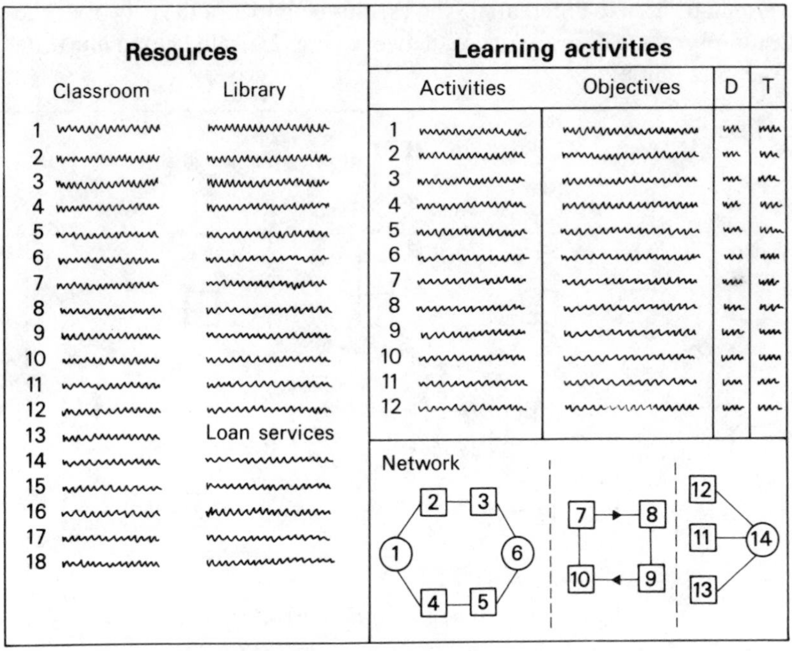

Resources		Learning activities			
Classroom	Library	Activities	Objectives	D	T

Network

Fig. 2.1 *The master plan*

classroom. The cooperation of the school librarian should be sought. If the library has a well-developed subject index as well as classified catalogue, the teacher's master plan could be made very informative indeed, and could include the following:

- Key words in the subject index for pupils engaged in open-ended research.
- Classified numbers for pupils enquiring in specific subject areas.
- A list of titles and authors, annotated so that the teacher can give specific and careful directions, if this is the need.

The right-hand page describes the *learning activities*. The network at the bottom (see Fig. 2.2) is designed to answer the question: what does the pupil do next?

Learning activities network

This is the teacher's *map* of the unit of study, showing where the class teaching is to take place, where individual work is appropriate, and where the possibilities of small-group work exists. It should also show the place of assessment tests and evaluation procedures. A simple key should be used to differentiate the various activities of the network. The example of a learning activities network (Fig. 2.2) will help to illustrate the possibilities.

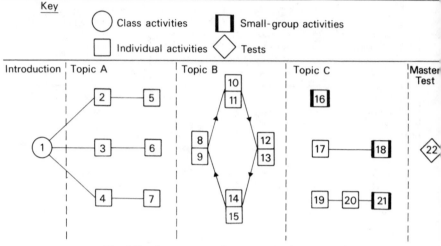

Fig. 2.2 *Patterns on a learning activities network*

Explanatory notes on Fig. 2.2

1. The vertical dashed lines separate the discrete parts of the study unit. In this example each of the parts is regarded as reasonably self-contained, not depending heavily on previous learning.
2. The introductory class activities are those concerned with rousing interest and providing an advance organizer (Table 1.5, Planning Document 4).
3. Where individual activities are on the same vertical they cover the same material, the higher positions representing the more difficult tasks.
4. In topic A the sequence is of two activities prepared at three levels of difficulty.
5. Topic B represents a 'circus' arrangement of four tasks at two levels of difficulty. Pupils can be started at any point and rotate through all four tasks.
6. Topic C involves small-group work, but the easier tasks involve some individual preparation as well.
7. The most important point about an activities network is that it encourages the teacher to start thinking about the logistics of classroom management at the *preparation stage*.

Calculating resource and task card requirements

Quantities of resources and task cards can be calculated, as shown in the two examples below.

1. If all pupils are to work sequentially through topics A, B, and C in that order their *minimum* requirements are as follows (assuming class size of 32):

    Tasks 2, 3, 4, 5, 6, and 7 = 11 copies of each
    Tasks 8, 9, 10, 11, 12, 13, 14, 15 = 4 copies of each
    Tasks 16, 17, 18, 19, 20, 21 = 11 copies of each

2. If topics A, B, and C are regarded as a circus, then *minimum* quantities are as follows:

    Tasks 2, 3, 4, 5, 6, and 7 = 4 copies of each
    Tasks 8, 9, 10, 11, 12, 13, 14, 15 = 2 copies of each
    Tasks 16, 17, 18, 19, 20, 21 = 4 copies of each

Recording the range of activities

The variations of a learning activities network are infinite. It is important, however, not to get too ambitious. Many teachers prefer to have a limited range of activities happening in their classrooms at any one time. They are aware of the dangers of 'information overload, cognitive overstimulation and decision stress'! (see Toffler, 1973).

Above the network there is a simple record of all the learning activities that have been prepared. The information could usefully include:

- the number of the activity;
- the title;
- the educational objectives;
- a rating for difficulty;
- a rating for the estimated length of time it will take.

It is important to note the following:

1. All activities are included: class teaching, group work, individual activities, tests. Some will have task cards, others will not. But the numbering sequence on the master plan must obviously be consistent with the numbering of the task cards.
2. The ratings for difficulty and time should be made subjectively by the teacher who prepares the task. The effort of making these judgements more precise and objective is usually not worth the time involved.

Preparing assessment tests

Many teachers will wish to rely heavily on a system of continuous assessment of their pupil's work. This is dealt with in chapter 7 which describes the management of individual learning. Continuous assessment is a vital part of a well-organized system of teaching. Tests are also essential, and the two types most likely to be used within a unit of study are mastery tests and final assessment tests.

Mastery tests

Mastery tests are best thought of as *exit permits* from one section of the unit to the next are for the information of the pupil as well as the teacher. For the pupil they provide feedback. They are really part of the learning experience, giving practice in what has been learnt, and giving confidence and reinforcement to the learner. They tell the pupil that the work has been mastered to a satisfactory *minimum* standard. For the teacher, the mastery tests help to identify a pupil's misconceptions and misunderstandings; and also to recognize the weaknesses in the design of the study unit.

Mastery tests should be designed to measure *minimum competence* and pupils should be taught to aim for full marks or nearly so. The tests could be self-administered and the results regarded as a piece of ephemeral information, useful for immediate discussion, but not part of the pupil's permanent record of achievement. A wise and generous use of mastery tests can have a beneficial effect on the motivation of all pupils.

Final assessment tests

A final assessment test provides an assessment of a different kind. It normally comes at the end of a unit and aims to provide a comprehensive assessment of each individual pupil's knowledge and understanding of the content of the unit. The questions are carefully selected. They need to:

- test the whole range of the subject matter;
- test the whole range of educational objectives adopted at the planning stage;
- discriminate between the different standards of performance achieved by the pupils.

Constructing the tests

Writing good mastery tests and a final assessment test is an important task in the preparation stage. Constructing tests is a big subject in its own right and only a brief introduction is attempted here. Readers are recommended to follow up some of the references in the bibliography, particularly Bloom: *Handbook of Formative and Summative Evaluation of Student Learning*, which provides an understanding of the thinking behind 'mastery learning' and mastery tests.

Objective test items

In both kinds of tests *objective* test items should play an important role. Such items are carefully structured and the marking is a routine clerical exercise with no demands made on the judgement of the marker. The types of objective test items are listed below.

True-false items   These are useful only for testing knowledge of specific facts and definitions.

Completion items   These are useful only for specific facts, definitions, and recognition of concepts. When only a *one* word answer is demanded the need for subjective judgement is removed. It is important that it is made clear to the pupil the *type* of word that is required.

Multiple choice items   These are very versatile and should be heavily used. They can be used to test a wide range of intellectual performance. They are not easy to devise, and a team involved in cooperative preparation should practice as much as possible and keep revising test items in the light of experience. Skill and speed can be achieved.

A good multiple choice question consists of

A STEM	and	FIVE POSSIBLE ANSWERS
(an incomplete statement which clearly presents a problem)		(only one of which clearly gives the best answer)

The following hints should help in their preparation:
1. Try to test higher intellectual skills as well as simple factual knowledge. Express the item in such terms that real application of learning is demanded.
2. Beware of building in clues to the right answer.
3. Include as much of the item as possible in the stem.

The following example of a multiple choice test item is used for testing application of knowledge at the end of a science study unit on specific heat.

Near the coasts and near large lakes it is observed that air temperatures do not change as rapidly as they do in areas far away from water. This is due to the fact that:

A. the water is always colder than the land surface;
B. the water is always warmer than the land surface;
C. the heavy rains of coastal areas affect the temperature;
D. the water warms and cools much more rapidly than the land;
E. the water warms and cools much more slowly than the land.

Subjective test items

Test items may also be *subjective*. These are often called the essay-type questions, but there is wide scope for requesting very short answers, such as a sentence or even a phrase, as well as full essays. The subjective test item is valuable for the testing of the skills of appraisal, organization, and synthesis. It is important to avoid straight demands for factual regurgitation. Think of the intellectual skills that are being tested and word the questions accordingly.

Finally, both mastery tests and final assessment tests should be examined critically in light of the planning documents for the study unit. Both the statement of objectives (Table 1.2, planning document 2) and the statement of content (Table 1.3, planning document 3) should be brought to bear.

Test instruments are never developed to perfection. They can be improved over a period of years by a thoughtful and well maintained team. The important thing is to make a start, however modest, as early as possible in the development of a course.

Preparing text and audio-visual materials for the teacher's use during class teaching

Good class teaching also demands thorough preparation. Class teaching is a vital part of the introductory phase in any study unit (see Planning Document 4, Table 1.5). It is concerned during this phase with arousing the pupil's awareness, imagination and interest, and giving them an advance organizer of the subject matter. But class teaching can also occur at later stages to help with difficult points, to coordinate, to organize the sharing of experiences, to give some new input.

Preparation for class teaching consists of:
1. Personal preparation.
2. The preparation of audiovisual aids.
3. The preparation of an accurate, comprehensive and balanced statement of the main ideas to be presented in the study unit.

Personal preparation

Personal preparation means acquiring a thorough knowledge of the subject matter. The really effective teacher in a class teaching situation is the one who has good subject knowledge, talks about it easily, uses vivid verbal illustrations, and draws on a wide repertoire of example, anecdote and significant detail. Preparing really well is a highly specialized research job, and inevitably teachers have to fall short of the ideal. This is the reason why many teams choose to operate team teaching, with the concept of the 'lead lesson' for which *one* teacher has prepared to an exceptional level for the benefit of several classes.

For the carrying out of this research it is almost impossible to give detailed advice which has wide applicability. However, the following suggestions might serve to indicate some useful lines of approach.

1. Conventional textbooks are not usually a good source. They are often highly condensed and the data is usually 'potted'.
2. Encyclopaedias are not usually good, for the same reasons.
3. 'Books for the School Library' (as listed by the educational publishers) are often rich sources of vivid and significant detail.
4. Biographers can provide material which will help the teacher *personalize* the message. Teaching can come alive when it is using real, named *people* as the mediators of knowledge and ideas.
5. Highly specialized adult material can often be very useful. It may need adaptation for school use. Sources of such material are government agencies, commercial, industrial and professional organizations, community organizations, newspapers and periodicals of all kinds.

No teacher will ever be satisfied with the results of this kind of research. The important thing is to make a start, to get away from the unthinking reliance on academic abstractions and generalizations.

Preparation of audio-visual aids

The second preparation task for class teaching is to prepare the audio-visual aids for the presentation. The choice is wide:

- schools television programmes (live or recorded);
- schools radio programmes (live or recorded);
- film;
- filmstrip;
- slides;
- overhead projection materials;
- audio-tape;
- records;
- the blackboard.

An important question for the teacher is to choose the right medium for each teaching job. Teachers who are particularly interested in this question should consult some of the specialized texts listed in the bibliography (Hanson, 1975; Romiszowski, 1974).

Statement of main ideas

The last job in the preparation of material for the class teaching is to write an accurate, comprehensive and balanced statement of the main ideas presented in the study unit. The purpose of this statement is to give the pupils an 'advance organizer' for the study unit. It can be thought of as a map and a guide to the new ground that is to be covered, giving the pupils a structure around which to organize their learning. Inevitably it has to be at a fairly high level of abstraction and some teachers may feel that this violates the principles of leading from the particular to the general, and from the concrete to the abstract. The answer is that children need both forms of support. The statement of main ideas is not something to be fully comprehended at the first encounter; it is rather a necessary reference document to be used frequently throughout the unit of study.

So the statement of main ideas needs a lot of thought. It should be written concisely and with an interesting layout of text, including headings and subheadings, underscoring and boxing. It must *look* good.

At the risk of offending some teachers with a 'progressive' commitment, the statement of main ideas should be *given* to the pupils. In this crucial task we cannot risk inaccuracies, imbalance or inadequacy, therefore pupils should copy it from the overhead projector screen or blackboard; alternatively they could have it as a printed handout. The statement should not be too long, for example a double page of the pupil's workbook is a good size, so that the whole can be seen at a glance.

Preparing a teacher's guide

This is necessary because all members of the team will not have been fully involved in all the preparatory activities. It helps, too, in reaffirming the purposes and styles that have been adopted for the study unit. The contents should be as follows:
1. The title and broad aims.
2. A statement of content and main ideas.

3. An explanation of the educational objectives which the study unit promotes.
4. A description of the individual learning activities with suggestions about further opportunities and likely problems.
5. A list of additional optional resources (e.g., library, loan services).
6. Suggestions about possible modifications and improvements.

Summary of preparation for a study unit

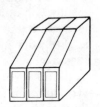

A boxed and numbered collection of resources.

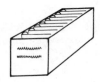

A set of task cards for individual and small-group use.

A master plan giving details of task cards and resources.

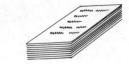

A series of assessment tests.

Audio-visual aids for use in teacher presentation.

A teacher's guide.

It looks like a formidable undertaking. It certainly is, if it is done thoroughly and completely, but as outlined below, *the advantages of systematic preparation of this kind are very substantial indeed.*

- It can be started in a modest and incomplete way, building up year by year in both size and sophistication.
- It lends itself to cooperation, and indeed *demands* it. When several are thinking, searching, and preparing in a collaborative way, they all gain. There are practical advantages, for example, the saving of time, the division of labour to make the best use of individual skills and interests. But there is also intellectual stimulation which can raise the level of work throughout the team.
- It pays off in the classroom. The really well-prepared teacher, backed by the resources and documentation described in this chapter, is in a very powerful position. Pupils have plenty of work, and they are thoroughly absorbed, while the teacher has some of the pressure taken away and can exercise much initiative, intervening in a purposeful and controlled way. Teacher–pupil relationships improve, because most of the interactions are personal and private. The classroom can change from a place of tensions and frustrations, to one of calm, quiet, purposeful work.

3. A Policy for Teaching

So far we have been concerned with what happens *before* the actual teaching commences, and we have given a little thought to the evaluation that takes place *after* the teaching. This is in line with much contemporary discussion. There are inputs that precede teaching, and outputs that result from it. The classroom is represented by a black box. Some people believe that if we manipulate the input variables we are doing all that is needed to bring about improvements in teaching. This view completely ignores *the processes that take place in the classroom*. The events and activities that occur there are accepted as secret and private, things that only concern the teacher and the pupils. It is believed that the work of the teacher will be improved by, for example, the evidence of research, curriculum development projects, in-service education, advice and inspection, or by more systematic evaluation of the outcomes of schooling. This may be so, but how exactly will it happen?

We need to get inside that black box, to look carefully at what happens there, and to relate it to the given inputs and to the desired outputs. We need to tackle the difficult job of defining what we mean by good teaching. There is no universal answer because perceptions and styles differ, and good teachers are not necessarily all alike. So where do we start? Surely each individual teacher must attempt his own definition. The definition can be a purely personal one, but it would be better if a team of cooperating teachers could initiate a debate in order to arrive at a group definition. If this was built on to a base of cooperative planning and preparation, the team would be in a very strong position indeed.

One use of a Policy for Teaching would be as a basis for an on-going debate. When a teacher or a group of teachers has made such a declaration then every piece of educational news, every report, every research finding, every new development can be examined in the light of the adopted Policy. Does it confirm the detailed intentions described within the Policy, or does it question or challenge some parts of it? Every new experience can be compared with the Policy. Does it confirm the detail of the Policy, or does it suggest that parts of the Policy are too ambitious or too unambitious, or just wrongly directed? The Policy becomes a stimulus to thinking.

The second main use of a Policy for Teaching is as a practical tool in the improvement of teaching. It is only by knowing clearly what it is we are aiming to achieve that we can *systematically* set about making improvements. The Policy is part of the value system within which a team or an individual works: it sets objectives, influences directions and styles, and provides a discipline for systematic endeavour.

How to Produce a Policy for Teaching

First, there must be a commitment to the idea. There must be the belief that the existence of a Policy can make a difference. Without this belief it is useless to proceed. Teachers who are new to the idea will need time to develop their awareness and interest before being asked to commit themselves. Persistence by the leader will pay off.

Second, it will be necessary to do a search of relevant literature. Teachers need help to gather together their ideas, and they need help in articulating the philosophy underlying their practices, many of which they perform intuitively. The advantage of theory is that it tells us quite precisely what we are already doing! Written sources can be government reports, HMI documents, research reports, curriculum development reports from bodies like the Schools Council, and specialist books for teachers. They should be scanned for answers to these questions:

● What does the writer of this book or document consider to be the attributes of good teaching?
● How does this apply in my particular field?

Ideas should be collected at first without any attempt at classification. This is a brainstorm to produce an unassorted heap of ideas and without any attempt to criticize or select. It will be the raw material for subsequent investigation and discussion. The very act of scanning and collecting should prove stimulating in itself. A list of possible sources is provided in the bibliography. (Barnes, 1971 and 1975; Clegg and Megson, 1968; Davies, 1980; DES, 1977 and 1978; Galton, Simon and Croll, 1980; Marland, 1975.)

Third, the local factors should now be considered. What school policies exist which have a bearing on the proposed Policy for Teaching? What styles, traditions and conventions are there which ought to influence the selections? What about the local context outside the school? Are there developments or initiatives with which the team would wish to be associated? Cooperation with groups of teachers from other schools can yield substantial benefits, and it is often worth 'joining' even when the cooperating group's intentions do not seem to match our own exactly.

Fourth, if working in a team, contributions from individual team members should now be invited. At this stage there is no need to impose a structure on these contributions but simply to regard them as 'free-expression', produced in note form as rough drafts. They are intended to add to the stock of ideas and opinions.

Fifth, the debate is ready to begin. But this is no academic exercise. The object is to produce a working document, in the hope that it really will prove to be of practical use. But the debate itself will be worth while in its own right because teachers need to talk about their classroom experiences, not in a trivial or anecdotal way, but in a systematic and disciplined way.

A classification of teaching activities

It is useful to have a classification system for the events and activities of teaching. It helps thinking and planning by sharpening the definitions and clarifying the value judgements that might otherwise remain obscure. It provides a common framework to support both theoretical knowledge and practical experience and intuition. In addition, by providing the basis for a language for talking about teaching, it helps to enable teachers to communicate with each other about the *technicalities* of classroom management. A teacher needs to be able to describe more precisely what takes place in the classroom so that techniques and systems can be subjected to critical analysis. A classification is a necessary step in the formulation of a Policy for Teaching.

Naturally, there are problems and dangers. Can we really expect agreement even among the members of a small team? Is there a danger that we shall become too prescriptive, too rigid, and unable to respond to the unintended and the unexpected? Is there a danger that we shall stifle thinking rather than stimulate it by forcing it into a predetermined mould? Is it really possible to categorize the enormous range and variety of the interactions that take place in a classroom? Is there a danger that in pursuit of *observable* events and activities we may end by completely trivializing the work of the classroom? These are real dangers, and it would be unwise to ignore them. But a Policy for Teaching should be seen as an imperfectly designed tool, something which can be improved after experience in using it. Because a tool is imperfect is in itself an insufficient reason for declining to make use of it. Life is too short to insist on perfection!

So we are looking at the actual events and activities in the classroom. What do the teachers and pupils do and how can we classify these events and activities?

Framework for the Policy

The following headings are suggested as an example for forming the framework of a Policy for Teaching.

The classroom

The physical layout of the furniture and equipment should form part of the Policy. Discussion should centre on the choice of equipment and on how it should be stored and used to best effect. Standards of cleanliness and tidiness can be determined, with particular reference to end-of-lesson routines. Where a room is shared among a number of teachers there should be agreement about the use of display space.

Planning and preparation

These important matters have already been the subject of Chapter 1, but they need to be included in the Policy for Teaching in order that the statement can be fully comprehensive. To recapitulate, the end products of thorough planning are:

- the basic facts that have a bearing on the study programme;
- the educational objectives that will serve as a guide and a checklist;
- the outline of content;
- the sequence of learning activities proposed;
- the arrangements for the evaluation of the study programme.

The end-products of the preparation phase are:

- an organized collection of resources;
- a collection of task cards giving guidance for individual and small-group work;
- a master plan detailing resources and tasks for use by the teacher;
- a series of assessment tests;
- the audio-visual aids likely to be required in teacher presentation;
- a teacher's guide.

Resources

A Policy for Teaching should be concerned with: the range and types of printed resources; the range and types of audio-visual resources; the storage and retrieval systems for the classroom resources; the arrangements for the use of resources beyond the classroom; the supply and storage systems for the stationery and the writing and drawing instruments.

The teacher as leader and presenter

The teacher plays an important role in all aspects of the work of the classroom, but this heading emphasizes the purely *personal* contributions. First, there are the personal attributes—the patience, the cheerfulness, the confidence, the self-control, the flexibility—all of which can help to make for successful teaching. Then, there are the technical competencies of presentation, including the techniques of exposition, questioning, discussion, leading. These in turn lead to questions of language and voice, and style in communication. The teacher's subject knowledge can also be taken under this heading: good understanding of the structure of the subject matter, a good repertoire of example, illustration, anecdote, and vivid detail.

The pupil: motivation and needs

This heading considers the pupil as an individual. The Policy for Teaching should say something about catering for individual differences. This should include not only cognitive differences, but also differences in emotional makeup, and differences resulting from social and cultural backgrounds. This is the place for a statement about the pupil's motivation, sense of achievement, feeling of recognition, willingness to participate, and a sense of responsibility.

The classroom as a social system

This is important because the classroom is more than a collection of individuals. How the class is organized for individual work, for small-group work, and for whole-class work is an important aspect of teaching policy. Such organization is an aspect about which there can be disagreement and this makes it all the more desirable that it should be thoroughly thought out in a rational and responsible way. A teacher who has thought deeply and has a commitment to a way of organization can usually make it work successfully. The structure and functions of groups also need to be clearly stated, particularly considerations of group size, group selections, group tasks, group discipline, and rules.

Personal relationships

Teacher and pupils relate to each other as people. While this is bound up with the business of teaching and learning, it is nevertheless worth considering as a separate dimension because it can be such a powerful influence for good or ill. We are concerned with personal warmth and affection, with approachability, and with responsiveness. Relationships need to be considered between teacher and pupil and between pupil and pupil.

Management of time

Time is the most precious commodity. Its allocation is fixed: we cannot usually beg, borrow, or steal any more. It is one of the hard facts of teaching in school that the pupil contact time is not usually capable of being increased. So time management is crucial to success and becomes an important component in a Policy for Teaching. Statements need to be made about the amount of time given to teacher–pupil interaction, and this can vary enormously both in quantity and quality. Research has confirmed that the amount of time given to 'substantive interaction' between the teacher and pupil is an important factor in pupil learning. In a similar way the amount of time a pupil spends actually on task, engaged in the academic learning that has been prescribed, is an indicator of likely success. This seems obvious enough, but organizational tasks, waiting, wasting time, and other non-academic activities can occupy a surprising amount of time. There is also the question of the balanced use of the teacher's time. The Policy for Teaching needs to determine the main types of teacher activity and work towards an ideal time allocation and time distribution.

Management and control

This is a complex set of tasks. It includes a lot more than the keeping of discipline, although that is an important element. The management and control functions also include the setting of objectives, the prescription of tasks, the guidance on task procedures, the monitoring functions, the feedback procedures, and the recording of important data about the pupils' work and progress. This is a view of the teacher as a controller: it is about information, about decisions, and about procedures.

Intellectual level

Finally, a Policy for Teaching should say something about the intellectual level of the verbal exchanges and the activities that take place in the classroom. It has been a consistent criticism of teaching, from both subjective and objective observation, that much of what takes place in the classroom is rote learning or is concerned only with the simplest forms of knowledge and understanding. The Policy for Teaching must declare itself and set standards that will enable teachers to respond to this criticism.

The presentation of a Policy for Teaching

It is to be hoped that the ten headings discussed in the last section will be studied as an example. It would be wrong to regard them as a prescription to suit all situations. Preferably, teachers should devise their own framework headings since substantial benefits are to be gained from the discussion involved in making the selection and in attempting a broad statement about each heading.

There is still more to do, for, in order to convert the Policy into a working document, we need to shift the language from the abstract to the concrete. What can you actually observe in a classroom which tells you that the teaching is good? What are the specific indicators that will express our Policy for Teaching in concrete terms? This is difficult to accomplish. A sensible balance has to be struck: on the one hand, it is desirable to have indicators that are both observable and incontrovertible; on the other hand, we must recognize that much observation in a classroom is bound to involve value judgements. So we must do the best we can, looking for the concrete observable indicator, but not forcing this in a way that goes against common sense and professional judgement. The number of possible indicators under any one heading is infinite. Therefore, since the number we use is an arbitrary one, let us choose ten for each heading, recognizing that we are seeking the ten *most significant* indicators of achievement in the general aims of our Policy for Teaching. The result will be a working document, which should take its place alongside the five developed in Chapter 1. So we shall call it planning document 6 (see Table 3.1), in order to establish its relationship with the others.

The indicators are personally chosen. They represent the author's view of what *he* would like an observer to see in *his* teaching. It is offered as an *example*, a model to study, not a prescription as to what constitutes good teaching. The message is, always, that the teacher needs to develop his own indicators.

Each part of the table is devoted to one heading and on each there is a general statement followed by ten indicators. Some overlap between the headings is inevitable.

The Policy for Teaching is a formidable document. It shows dramatically what a demanding and complex business we are in. No individual teacher can hope to achieve perfection. But the Policy for Teaching sets the goal. It is a goal none of us will ever reach in full measure but we must forever seek it.

Table 3.1 *The Policy for Teaching*

PLANNING DOCUMENT 6

The classroom
The classroom has an attractive appearance. It is functional, having regard to its main purpose and to its practical effectiveness.

1. The room is clean and tidy, occupied only by equipment and materials currently in use.

2. Wall displays are attractively arranged and are relevant to the current teaching and learning.

3. Relevant reading and reference material is available to pupils at all times, without the need to request it.

4. The layout of furniture gives pupils as much working space as possible, and allows for flexibility between individual work, small-group work, and class teaching.

5. There is an adequate supply of all the writing and drawing materials and equipment that pupils are likely to require.

6. The resources for learning currently in use are stored in such a way as to permit quick retrieval.

7. Adequate equipment is available to permit the projection of slides and filmstrips, and the playback of audio-tapes.

8. When required, there is access to TV, radio, and an overhead projector.

9. There are clear policies, rules, and procedures relating to the shared use of the room by several teachers.

10. There are arrangements to ensure the proper use of furniture, equipment, and materials at times when teaching is not taking place.

Planning and preparation
There is evidence of sound planning based on a rigorous analysis of the needs of the situation. This is backed by detailed and thorough preparation.

1. There is a clear statement about the rationale of the programme of learning: needs, context, and general aims.

2. A statement of educational objectives is available to serve as a guide or a checklist.

3. There is a summary of the content of the programme with a justification.

4. There is a description of the kinds of learning activities thought to be appropriate at each stage in the programme.

5. Explicit arrangements for the evaluation of the programme are available.

6. There is a well-chosen and well-organized collection of resources.

7. Some guidance for pupils has been prepared in advance in order to take pressure off the teacher during class time.

8. Documents are available to the teacher to help in classroom management (examples: A Teacher's Guide, A Teacher's Master Plan).

9. Prepared tests are available for use.

10. There is a good stock of teacher presentation materials, e.g., audio-visual aids, copies of significant texts.

Resources
The classroom has resources of sufficient quantity, quality, and variety in order to give maximum support to the teaching programme.

---

1. Quantities of individual resource items are matched to the needs of the programme (class sets/small sets/individual copies).

2. Printed resources have design appeal, in addition to providing the necessary data and stimuli.

3. There is a sufficient variety of printed resources to match the reading capabilities of all pupils in the class.

4. Resources are classified and stored in a way that facilitates use by the pupils.

5. There is adequate support for pupils' learning through visual and aural aids: pictures, line drawings, maps and diagrams, audio and visual tapes.

6. There is further support for pupils' learning through the availability of concrete objects such as specimens, models, artefacts.

7. Pupils have plenty of opportunities to promote their learning through direct contact with the resources rather than relying exclusively on the mediation of the teacher.

8. There are explicit arrangements for the pupils' use of the central library/resources centre provision.

9. Contacts with local providers of resources are well established.

10. The teacher has access to comprehensive sources of information (e.g., publishers' catalogues, development project prospectuses) about resources available to support his work.

The teacher as leader and presenter

The teacher exhibits the personal attributes, the technical competencies, and the subject knowledge that will promote pupils' learning in an atmosphere of respect and confidence.

1. The teacher's mood is normally patient and good humoured.

2. The teacher demonstrates both in word and in action a feeling of self-confidence and a high degree of self-control.

3. Flexibility and a creative response to events are demonstrated by the teacher.

4. The teacher's instructions, descriptions, and explanations are brief and clear.

5. As discussion leader, the teacher's skills result in a high level of pupil participation which is rational, responsible, and authentic.

6. The teacher demonstrates the skills of effective questioning so that the level of pupil thinking is raised.

7. The teacher's voice is used in a manner that is varied, interesting, and encouraging.

8. The language used by the teacher is varied and encouraging.

9. The teacher always demonstrates a sound understanding of the structure of the subject matter.

10. The teacher draws on a large repertoire of example, illustration, anecdote, and vivid detail.

The pupil: motivation and needs

The teaching shows consideration for the pupils as individuals. There is evidence of a sense of achievement, a feeling of recognition, a willingness to participate, and a sense of responsibility.

1. The teacher demonstrates the skill of adaptation to the full range of intellectual differences within the class.

2. The teacher responds to differences in personality and emotional makeup.

3. The teacher demonstrates an awareness of social and cultural differences, and an ability to adjust to these with sensitivity.

4. Pupils exhibit a sense of pride in their work.

5. There is adequate recognition of pupils' individual achievements through praise and through the work being taken seriously.

6. Pupils exhibit a willingness to participate in the thinking and activities of the lesson.

7. A sense of responsibility is shown by pupils in all aspects of their work and behaviour.

8. Pupils are frequently asked to voice their own perceptions of their needs.

9. There are opportunities for an individual pupil to talk privately with the teacher.

10. Criticism by the teacher is, for the most part, conducted in private.

The classroom system
The teaching is organized so as to create opportunities for pupils to work in groups and to gain benefit from the group experience.

1. Pupils experience a *balance* of teaching and activities, organized as a whole class, in small groups, in pairs, and as individuals.

2. There is the opportunity for pupils to work in pairs for the purpose of collaboration on convergent tasks.

3. Pupils have the opportunity to work in small groups for the purpose of sharing experiences, for competing, and for problem solving.

4. Pupils have the opportunity to work as members of the whole class in order to share common experiences and to enjoy a sense of unity.

5. Small-group size is large enough to produce some diversity of response, yet small enough to ensure participation of all members.

6. There is evidence that the composition of the groups has been determined (whether by the teacher or by the pupils themselves) in relation to their function.

7. There is evidence of a wide range of tasks performed in groups: problem solving, games and simulations, discussions.

8. The teacher offers adequate guidance to pupils on the procedures for group work.

9. All group work is conducted in a disciplined manner.

10. There are clear procedures for groups to report the outcomes of their work.

Personal relationships
Teachers and pupils enjoy each other's company, are mutually supportive, and treat each other with courtesy and respect.

1. The teacher shows a personal interest in individual pupils for their own sake, beyond the needs of the immediate learning process.

2. The teacher actively fosters a sense of group cohesion in work and in discipline.

3. The teacher uses the conventional adult courtesies in conversation with pupils.

4. Pupils feel free to signal their difficulties and to alert the teacher to organizational mistakes and problems.

5. Pupils work together cooperatively and willingly on common projects.

6. The teacher makes frequent use of praise and encouragement for individual efforts.

45

7. The teacher frequently accepts a pupil's expression of feeling.

8. The teacher frequently accepts or uses ideas expressed by a pupil.

9. Pupils sometimes disagree with the teacher in a mature and nonthreatening manner.

10. Teacher and pupils occasionally share a sense of humour.

The management of time

Teacher and pupils get most out of the time available through a well-developed sense of priorities and a sense of economy in the expenditure of time.

1. The teacher allocates a high proportion of the available time to academic work.

2. The pupils spend a high proportion of their time actually engaged on their tasks.

3. The pupils experience a high degree of success during their engaged time.

4. The teacher maintains a good balance in the use of time on supervisory, organizational, and teaching tasks.

5. A high proportion of the teacher's time is spent in 'substantive interaction' with his pupils, (i.e., explaining, questioning, describing, illustrating).

6. The teacher has eliminated unnecessary routines and activities from his own performance.

7. The teacher has delegated (to ancillaries or pupils) responsibilities and tasks that are within their competence.

8. Simple and speedy procedures have been devised by the teacher for tackling routine events and recurring problems.

9. There is evidence that the teacher plans ahead so that time in lessons is used most effectively.

10. The teacher regularly reviews the conduct of lessons in terms of the effective use of time by himself and by the pupils.

Management and control

The teacher operates an efficient system of management and control. This rests on firm arrangements and on appropriate procedures.

1. An efficient system for the continuous recording of each pupil's tasks, progress, and achievements is available.

2. The teacher establishes clear personal objectives and commitments for each pupil.

3. The teacher has established procedures for the monitoring of each pupil's work.

4. Feedback is given to the pupil so that he has a good knowledge about his own performance.

5. The teacher gives clear directions on task procedures and encourages pupils to understand the structure of the lesson and of the course.

6. The pupils are encouraged to help in decision-making about the organization of the work.

7. The teacher handles minor lapses in pupils' behaviour in a competent way, demonstrating alertness, sure judgement, and confidence.

8. The teacher copes with the complexities of classroom life (many different things happening at the same time) in a calm and confident way.

9. The flow of classroom activities is maintained by the teacher, particularly at times of transition.

10. The teacher uses positive reinforcement (praise, incentives, peer manipulation) to help overcome problems caused by a difficult or disturbed pupil.

Intellectual level
The teacher constantly strives to raise the intellectual level of the verbal exchanges and the activities which take place in the classroom.

1. The teacher allows time for pupils to express their ideas and to expand on them.

2. The teacher sets a good example as a user of higher levels of thought.

3. Encouragement is given to pupils who attempt to express themselves in abstract terms.

4. The teacher phrases questions in ways which will provoke divergent responses from the pupils.

5. The teacher encourages an awareness among the pupils of their own thought processes.

6. Pupils demonstrate a willingness to analyse knowledge and ideas.

7. The pupils demonstrate a capacity for developing hypotheses and testing them.

8. A readiness is shown by pupils to criticize information and ideas in a rational and responsible way.

9. Pupils are not afraid to express value judgements and to have them discussed.

10. Pupils constantly seek to structure their knowledge and understanding in a meaningful way.

4. The leadership of the team

Leadership is important for the success of a teaching team. However, there is no universal prescription for successful leadership for it depends very much on the situation and on the people in the team. And it is a good team which recognizes that leadership can and should come from every single member, depending on the logic and the needs of situations. So while a chapter on leadership may be particularly directed at the formally designated job holder, it also has messages for every team member who will be called upon to lead from time to time.

Leadership used to be equated with issuing commands and supervising their execution. It was assumed that strong personality and 'charisma' were the necessary attributes. These are as important today as they were in the past, but modern thinking also emphasizes a humble and self-effacing role for leadership. It is not so much concerned with the outward manifestations of leadership as with its actual achievements exemplified by the success of the team as a whole, a philosophy that is by no means new.

> The best of all rulers is but a shadowy presence to his subjects,
> Next comes the ruler they love and praise;
> Next comes the one they fear;
> Next comes the one with whom they take liberties.
> When there is not enough faith, there is lack of good faith.
> Hesitant, he does not utter words lightly.
> When his task is accomplished and his work done,
> The people all say, 'It happened to us naturally'.
> (Lao Tzu)

The idea of a 'natural' or 'born' leader has great appeal, and there is no doubt that some individuals appear to lead effortlessly. They are fortunate, but the rest of us need not despair. Much can be accomplished by a thoughtful analysis, and that is the purpose of this chapter.

The role of a leader can be described under seven main headings.

1. *Establishing aims and objectives*   The clear definition of the purposes of the team and the kinds of results that are sought.
2. *Establishing sound structures*   The division of labour, the lines of communication and answerability.
3. *Communications*   The fostering of good knowledge, understanding, and shared values among the members of the team.

4. *Motivation* The fostering of the will to work and succeed through the careful consideration of the individual's personal needs.
5. *Development* The systematic processes of training and experience by which individuals grow in knowledge, skills, insights, and attitudes.
6. *Evaluation* The systematic collection of information and judgements about the performance of the team in all aspects of its work.
7. *Leadership* The leadership of intellect and of action, particularly at times of great opportunity and at times of crisis.

Each heading will be discussed in turn, particularly from the point of view of the improvement of teaching.

Establishing aims and objectives

We have already looked at the use of educational objectives in course planning but the aims and objectives adopted by a teaching team need to embrace many other aspects of school life. It is best to think of aims and objectives simply as desired *achievements*. Aims are fundamental, long term, and expressed in general terms while objectives are more practical, short term, and stated more precisely.

Thinking will always start with the pupils. What do we want them to achieve? What differences do we hope to see in their knowledge, understanding, use of intellectual skills, and in their intellectual and social maturity? What kind of experiences and activities should they have in order to bring about these changes?

Inevitably, the team will be drawn into discussion about intermediate objectives, i.e., achievements which are simply regarded as steps in the right direction towards ultimate goals. Examples of such intermediate objectives might be:

● to establish and operate a school bookshop;
● to promote exchange visits with a school on the continent;
● to establish a voluntary special-interest club in after-school hours.

None of these, in themselves, will *necessarily* bring about desired changes in the pupils (the pupils may not read the books, they may develop hostility towards their host school on the continent, or they may misuse the facilities offered by the club). But it is a reasonable assumption that, given careful management, each of these intermediate objectives should prove to be a useful step towards ultimate goals.

The main difficulty in using an objectives approach is that the work of the teacher is complex and a very large number of objectives are required to do it justice. So a team which attempts to make an explicit statement

49

to cover all its objectives will have a huge task, and the whole exercise could easily become counter-productive. The secret of success is to be selective, and to concentrate team efforts, accepting that the objectives are being used to make changes or to bring about improvements, not merely to describe what is already being done. This selective approach requires five steps.

1. The team discusses its *broad aims* and agrees a written statement (probably no longer than one side of A4 paper). The statement is reviewed once a year to determine any changes or extensions.

2. For each school year one or two *key areas* for specific change or improvement are selected. Where are this year's big problems? What new opportunities are likely to present themselves? Here are some examples of possible key areas.

- course planning
- resources preparation
- pupils' discipline
- assessment and records
- use of external advice and support
- pupils' service to the community
- continuity in pupils' education
- teaching methods
- pupils' work standards
- course evaluation

3. Within each of the chosen key areas the team now writes a small number of objectives. This requires great care and the following points should be considered:

- make sure everyone is involved in the thinking;
- choose a small number of objectives that are significant and likely to make a real difference;
- make sure that each objective is big enough to be challenging without being impossible;
- write it down as precisely as possible, specifying *who* is going to do *what*, *when*, and *where*.

4. Finally, the team publishes its objectives in order to demonstrate its own commitment and to get support from other people outside the team.

The 'Management by Objectives' approach can be of immense value. It concentrates thinking, gives a sense of common purpose, and encourages a collaborative style of working. Such a spirit spreads; it is often observed that the management style of a team of teachers is reflected in the style adopted by individual teachers in their classrooms, and the pupils are influenced by it too.

Establishing sound structures

Even within a small team of teachers, sound structures can have a beneficial effect. Consider the differences between the two systems of organization outlined in Table 4.1.

Table 4.1 *Comparison between two systems of organization*

	Style A	Style B
Authority	The team leader assumes a respect for and obedience to his authority at all times.	Authority is more generally distributed. Personal knowledge in a given situation determines who is leader.
Selection of staff	Formal. Based on qualifications and experience. 'Scientific' selection.	Informal. Sometimes adventurous, preferring someone who might stimulate rather than conform.
Job description	Clearly defined. Resorted to in times of dispute.	General and flexible.
Chain of command	Through 'official' channels. Vertical.	Emphasizes collaboration, communication, and consultation. Horizontal.
Rules and procedures	Laid down in detail in order to guarantee standardized responses and styles.	Minimal and flexible. The 'logic of the situation'.
Records and reports	Heavily used.	*Ad hoc* rather than routine.

'A' is the 'bureaucratic' style. Its critics say that it stifles initiative, that power-seekers rather than creative people prosper. On the other hand, it offers stability because people know where they stand and what is expected of them. 'B' is the 'organic' style. Its supporters claim that it provides a more creative and stimulating environment, better able to adapt to change, and that it encourages individuals to develop their talents. On the other hand, it can produce an uncomfortable environment in which to work since there is a lack of certainty and stability and this can lead to chronic insecurity.

It is best not to go overboard for either system. 'Bureaucratic' styles are probably best for routine 'housekeeping' and maintenance tasks, like care of rooms, general discipline of the pupils, the management of stock, the keeping of pupils' records. 'Organic' styles are probably more appropriate when planning new courses, experimenting with new methods, or planning a programme for the improvement of teaching.

It is not easy to operate different styles within one team, and much explanation and education will be required so that team members can appreciate the benefits of this 'contingency' style of management. The ideas need to be communicated to the pupils too. They need to be able to distinguish between those occasions when rules are to be obeyed without question, and those when active questioning and the development of individual styles are desirable.

Communications

This is a major concern to all organizations, large and small, and it is a frequent cause of dissatisfaction in our schools. This is serious because teachers need good communications with their pupils, with each other, and with the outside world, if they are to do their job properly.

The probable cause of our failures in communication is that we have not yet abandoned some misconceptions. First, we have tended to think that communication is a one-way process, and that the direction is from the top downwards. If only we could speak or write more clearly, or more frequently, we would have no difficulty in getting our pupils or our subordinates to understand. The trouble with this belief is that it fails to recognize just how threatening *all* downward communication is. The good leader spends time listening to those under him, tries to understand their point of view, helps them clarify their thinking, and encourages them to be adaptable by sharing information and experience, and by setting an example. Communication begins where the receiver is.

Second, we have believed that more communication means better communication, for example, whenever the charge of 'lack of communications' is made, we establish another noticeboard, install another telephone extension, institute another standing committee, or insist on more paper work, in the belief that all will come right. But sometimes these tactics can make matters worse. Many teachers in our schools suffer from 'information overload', a problem resulting from the availability of too much unrelated and unsorted information. The good leader, instead of increasing the amount of information, helps people to cope effectively by careful selection, good timing, and an economical use of words both written and spoken.

Third, we have assumed that communication is only concerned with information. But most 'failures in communication' are really failures in understanding and in empathy, solutions to which might be found by spending more time trying to share each other's objectives, understandings, and values. Of course, the information problem is a real one but much can be accomplished by establishing an 'information base', where all information likely to be needed by members of the team is efficiently stored for easy access. This can avoid much information-passing which is time-consuming and inefficient, and should be confined to matters that are urgent or confidential.

Fourth, we have depended too much on language as the exclusive medium for communication. Teachers, who are proficient in the use of non-verbal communication in the classroom, often fail to recognize its value in their relationships with colleagues. What we *do* and how we *behave* are more powerful and enduring communicators than anything we may say or write. Ivan Illich referred to the 'testimony of action', and the 'eloquence of silence'.

Motivation

Teachers are accustomed to the problems of motivation through their work with their pupils. The problems are the same when dealing with colleagues. Motivation is an elusive thing; it is so intensely personal that it is difficult to offer general prescriptions.

Most research in the subject deals with hierarchies of need, beginning first with physical survival: food, warmth, shelter, rest. Social acceptance comes second: affection, security, companionship, respect from others. Self-esteem comes last: independence, self-respect, recognition, and achievement. The physical and social needs are basic, and until these are satisfied there is only a small drive to fulfil the needs of self-esteem. The responsibility of a leader at any given time is to attend to the needs of an individual *at the appropriate level.*

Teachers are accustomed to dealing with pupils whose basic physical and social needs are not being adequately met. For professional colleagues the needs are more usually those of the third level, and sometimes the organization can be guilty of failing to respond. All the highest levels of motivation are associated with the nature of the work itself. This means that all teachers must be helped to share a feeling of individual worth within the organization, to exercise a degree of independence in their work, to have their work known and appreciated by others. Above all they must succeed for 'nothing succeeds like success'!

This is an ideal state of affairs, and it requires some luck as well as good management to achieve it. Nevertheless, it is a vision worth striving for.

Development

The current emphasis on staff development is a recognition that the teacher is the most costly resource within the education service. It is also a recognition that a period of initial training for a teacher cannot possibly sustain him throughout a whole career with society and technology in such a state of rapid change. The detailed purposes of staff development can be presented from the individual's point of view and from the team's point of view. For the individual a programme of staff development helps the teacher to be more effective, to broaden his experience, to keep up to date, and to contribute on a wider front. For the team, it helps it to be more responsive to change and creates a reservoir of knowledge, skills, and experience which can be of immense benefit at times of new opportunities or crisis.

Outlined below are three propositions for a team's staff development programme with a brief justification of each.

The staff development programme should focus on the individual teacher

People have different needs and their needs change during the course of a career. The teacher should be encouraged to make his own proposals and have the regular opportunity to discuss them at length with the team leader.

The staff development programme should aim to integrate the development needs of the individual teacher with the needs of the team as a whole

This can lead to the highest levels of job satisfaction, giving an understanding of the value of the job and a feeling of real purpose in the acquisition of new knowledge and understanding.

The staff development programme should be accomplished through a wide range of experiences

Staff development is not just about going on courses, although that is a very important component. It is also about guided reading, systematic observation, systematic investigations, planned visits, contrived experiences, committee membership, and conference participation. The role of the team leader is crucial. He has the responsibility of bringing together three elements: knowledge and sympathetic understanding of the individual members of the team; the opportunities for training and new experiences; and the needs of the team as a developing and improving part of a whole school.

Evaluation

Most teachers will now agree that some form of evaluation is a necessary part of the life of a teacher but many shrink from the task because it seems enormous, never-ending, and bristling with difficulties. It is the team leader's responsibility to encourage the team to make a start and to protect them from the negative criticism so often directed towards initial attempts at evaluation.

There are four main questions to be answered:

- What is the purpose of the evaluation?
- What exactly is to be evaluated?
- Who is going to do it?
- How is it going to be done?

What is the purpose of the evaluation?

There are so many possible purposes that, even with massive help, a team cannot hope to cover them all on any one occasion. Selection of purpose is therefore necessary. The evaluation may be:

- to assess the performance of individual teachers;
- to assess the performance of pupils;
- to judge the merit and effectiveness of a course or programme of study;
- to make judgements about the learning resources in use;
- to provide a comprehensive report to higher authority.

What exactly is to be evaluated?

Whatever main purpose is chosen it will next be necessary to define the area in much more detail. What are the things we are looking for? What are the *indicators*? An example of the definition of an area in this way is the Policy for Teaching described in Chapter 3. Its scope is very wide, but any one of its headings could be developed into a full-scale evaluation study in its own right.

Who is going to do it?

This question raises still more questions. Is the initiative, direction, and implementation to be vested in someone external to the team, or is the evaluation to be regarded as an *internal* matter? Should the evaluation be *imposed* on the team, or should it be regarded as a participative exercise? Who makes judgements about whom? Is it only a top-down process, or do the juniors get an opportunity to discuss the work of their superiors? Apart from these general questions, there is a wide range of personnel who could and probably should be involved in the evaluation:

- the teachers themselves
- the pupils
- school governors
- community members
- local authority advisers
- college and university tutors
- colleagues from within the school
- colleagues from other schools
- the senior management team of the school.

How is it going to be done?

The best advice that can be given is to get started as soon as possible in a small and simple way. Attempts to devise a sophisticated system at the outset are likely to cause interminable discussion, a loss of confidence, and little real achievement. A start can be made by simply using the impressions and opinions of the team members themselves, a form of evaluation that is mostly subjective and entirely internal. Each member could be asked to write his own responses to a series of questions which would then form the basis of a group discussion. It is wise to define quite clearly what is being evaluated and for what purpose, and then to structure the discussion carefully by means of a predetermined agenda. A team that has successfully completed a simple evaluation of this kind will gain in confidence, and be ready to experiment with additional sources and techniques. But again, it is important not to try to add too much at once. The following possible techniques might be used:

- pupils' test results;
- questionnaires followed up by interviews (with pupils, staff team members, etc.);
- ratings based on agreed checklists;
- systematic observation based on agreed 'agendas' (see Chapter 12);
- involvement of external experts in all the above;
- comparisons with national data (where available), e.g., external examination results.

The subject of evaluation is too big to be properly handled in a short section such as this. Some further references are given in the bibliography. It is hoped that a team committed to the improvement of its teaching will make an *early start* on evaluation activities related to the whole of its work as a team.

Leadership

The chapter heading is used here as a topic heading in order to emphasize the 'first over the top' responsibilities of the team leader. So much of what has been written under the previous headings has shown a preference for the humble, self-effacing style, leading from the middle or behind. This has dominated much recent thinking about the management of organizations, both large and small. However, there are times and situations when the leader should clearly be out in front.

A good leader offers intellectual leadership. Many teachers will slip all too easily into belief and practice which emphasizes the expedient and the pragmatic, implying that the art of teaching is some kind of superior common sense. The team leader should aim to correct the balance by emphasizing the mutual support between theory and practice. This means trying to keep abreast of what is happening in educational research, in curriculum development both at local and national level. This is a tall order. The response should not be a total withdrawal from the scenes of action into the study, but rather a conscious effort to establish and maintain personal contacts with researchers, developers, university and college personnel. These people can help keep one abreast of developments on a wide front, advise on sources of information, and suggest lines of inquiry and further study that are economic in the use of precious time. The leader who uses his intellect also sets an example to his colleagues. The team benefits not only from the support of his personal knowledge, but also from the members' own following of his example. The team has become a *thinking team*.

A good leader steps forward in times of crisis and in times of great opportunity. The first demands courage to protect team members and to take the knocks oneself. The second demands a spirit of adventure and a willingness to expose one's ideas and actions to criticism. At times of uncertainty the team leader must expect to put forward the first rough proposals and expect also to have them rigorously criticized. This courageous act can frequently overcome a lot of hesitancy within the team.

Summary

The management responsibilities of a team leader are heavy and complex, especially as they have invariably to be discharged in addition to a full teaching load. They are nevertheless crucial. No programme for the improvement of teaching is likely to make much headway if the team does not exhibit the characteristics of a well-managed team:

- a clear vision of shared objectives;
- well-defined job responsibilities within a well-defined structure;
- a confidence about internal communications;
- a widespread feeling of personal involvement and satisfaction in the work of the team;
- a sense of personal and professional growth in each of the team members;
- a rigorous search for improvement in all aspects of the team's work through systematic review and evaluation;
- a leader who demonstrates his commitment in courageous and adventurous ways.

Part Three Classroom management

This section shifts the attention away from the planning and support of the team of teachers towards the efforts of the individual teacher in his own classroom. This is the 'sharp end' of the education system. The section analyses the actual events and activities of the classroom and makes suggestions for improvements. The use of the term 'classroom management' emphasizes the diverse and complicated nature of the teacher's classroom work.

5. Preparing the classroom

This chapter is about the classroom itself: the space, the furniture, the fittings, the equipment, and the physical layout of all these components. Not many teachers these days get the opportunity to design the rooms in which they will work, and the majority have to be content with what they are given. In most schools this amounts to a conventional classroom, usually nearly square in shape, with sides of between seven and eight metres. All the discussion in this chapter will be about such basic provision. This is not, in any way, an acceptance that such a classroom is the optimum but there is no point in developing ideas about the use of space which teachers simply do not have. If your classroom is bigger, or more imaginatively designed, no doubt you will be able to develop the ideas of this chapter for your own situation.

The organization of space

We need space for two main purposes: work and storage. The programmes of activities advocated in this book make heavy demands on both, so we must look carefully and critically at the whole question of space. Consider the traditional layout of many small classrooms. For example, in Fig. 5.1 it is clear that the workspace situation is desperate. The pupils are packed like sardines and the scope for flexible working arrangements are limited. No wonder that teachers working in such situations prefer the pupils to remain in their places! The trouble is that the teacher's legitimate need for storage space has been allowed to take priority over the pupils' need for work space. So the first objective in room planning must be to *get the right balance between work space and storage space*. In too many classrooms space is allocated to storage and is then not fully used: it would be better converted to work space. But suppose that the storage space has been cut down and what remains is performing a necessary and useful function. The answer is that more space must be *found*. An overcrowded classroom is so hostile to the improvement of teaching that desperate measures are called for!

Found space

The ideal solution would be a large purpose-built store room or cupboard fairly near to the classroom, but if no such opportunity exists

Fig. 5.1 *A traditional classroom layout*

then the alternative must be explored. Proposals will have to be formulated carefully; corridors or cloakrooms may offer hope, but problems like traffic flow will have to be considered. Nevertheless many older schools (prewar and immediate postwar) have enormous spaces which could be converted. Possibilities which should be investigated are:

- convert a spare cloakroom bay into additional workspace or store room;
- build high-level shelving above cloak racks for storage of bulky materials not immediately needed;
- move any slim, lockable cupboards to just outside the classroom door;
- if the corridor is wide enough, give it a table or bench which the pupils can use for noisy or dirty space-consuming activities.

The space-conscious teacher is always on the lookout for space that is not being fully used which could help solve classroom space problems. The principle is to banish from the classroom all bulky items which need to be stored but are not needed in the immediate future. If really necessary such items could be stored some way from the classroom. We need the equivalent of the domestic attic or the cellar!

In some classrooms the size of the furniture used is out of all proportion to the size of the room, and while the pupils have the benefit of large work surfaces they cannot be flexible in their work because of shortage of free space.

The redistribution of space

Looking back at Fig. 5.1 it appears that the pupils were packed tightly in the centre of the room, the periphery being occupied by side benches with cupboards, by free-standing cupboards and by the teacher's desk. What is the effect of this arrangement? It is that pupil movement becomes difficult and disruptive, the rearrangement of furniture becomes a hazardous and chaotic manoeuvre, and the teacher feels locked in a particular style of classroom management from which there is no escape.

Fig. 5.2 *The 'dining room' layout*

So let us imagine that we have resolved to break free of this restrictive layout. We shall want to support individual and paired work, and small-group work, and still retain the option to organize teaching and learning on a whole-class basis. Many teachers, committed to less formal methods, have adopted a 'dining-room layout', as shown in Fig. 5.2. Their intention is that this will encourage pupils to discuss their work with each other. It certainly does this, but it has weaknesses.

- Some pupils have their backs to the teacher which is slightly awkward during any sustained period of class teaching.
- During periods of individual work pupils may be distracted by others.

An alternative layout which has proved very effective is shown in Fig. 5.3. The room is the same size as that in Fig. 5.1 and the pupils' furniture is the same. This layout demonstrates some of the principles involved.

Fig. 5.3 *The 'peripheral' layout*

- All pupils can see the teacher and be seen.
- All pupils can see the projection screen and blackboard by moving without too much turning.
- The pupils occupy the periphery; the resources are in the centre. This means that resource-seeking expeditions are short and direct, with the minimum of disturbance for others.
- The furniture can serve well for individual study or collaboration in pairs. Pupils face a wall or a partition.
- The furniture can be quickly adapted for small-group work by removing partitions or by a small rearrangement of desks.
- The large space in the centre of the room containing the resource islands can be quickly and easily cleared for whole-class discussions, for drama, or for practical activities requiring space.

These are substantial advantages and it is worth a lot of effort to achieve them. Of course, dimensions and shapes of rooms vary; doors, windows, radiators, all present problems. Much trial and error is needed to determine the optimum layout for any one room. Cooperation is also required among all the users of a room. The principle of pupils on the periphery and resources in the centre is well worth trying.

Adaptations to furniture

Again there is likely to be little opportunity to specify the best type of furniture. Single locker desks or dual tables seem to be the most common provision. These can be surprisingly flexible.

Since our plans assume a fair amount of individual work it is worth while trying to improve the conditions for it. The purpose-built carrel or study booth immediately springs to mind. This cuts out distractions and creates a private world which encourages concentration and thoughtful reflection. Rather than buying the specially-made carrels, which are not only expensive but also heavy and somewhat inflexible in use, it is probably better to have some simple partitions made from 12.5 mm chipboard, a standard sheet of which cut in half will make two partitions measuring 1.2 × 1.2 m. The partition stands upright between a pair of dual tables, or between two pairs of single locker desks. For safety purposes the edges of the partitions should be smoothed and rounded or lipped with plastic. The arrangement is safe under normal use but tying the table legs together will make absolutely sure that the movement of a table will not cause the board to fall over. The advantage of the simple unfixed board is that it can easily be removed to convert a pair of study booths into one large table for small-group work.

The central resources area

The central resources area houses the resources that are in *current* use. It should be thought of as a cluster of 'resource islands' around which pupils can circulate on their resource-seeking expeditions. The islands must be easily removed to allow for alternative uses of this valuable space, so they should either be small and light or they should be on castors. Some commercially made trolleys are excellent for the purpose, being sturdy and easily moved while at the same time offering alternative shelving arrangements, but they tend to be expensive and homemade purpose-built units using Dexion or similar materials can be effective and cheap.

Contents of resource islands

The items that make up the contents of the resource islands are outlined below.

Specific to the current unit of study

These are mainly printed and typed/handwritten items:
* a boxed and numbered collection of printed resources;
* a boxed and numbered collection of non-print resources;
* a boxed set of task cards for individual and small group use;
* a boxed and numbered series of assessment tests;
* a collection of reference books appropriate to the study unit and to the age group of the pupils.

For general use in individual study

These items should be available to enable the pupil to satisfy his requirements without having to bother the teacher:
* a bank of stationery;
* a collection of writing instruments and drawing equipment;
* a collection of general reference books;
* a collection of audio-visual hardware suitable for individual or small-group work.

So many experiments in resource-based learning have foundered because of a failure to recognize these needs, and teachers have been forced into the role of issuing clerk. The frequently made claim of being a 'manager of resources' is an attempt to justify this wasteful use of professional time.

Careful thought should be given to the detail of the components of the resource islands. The collections need to be comprehensive, and yet finely tuned to local conventions. For example, some teachers may feel it necessary to provide a pen for each pupil; others, in more favourable situations, will find it sufficient to provide only a small number, to overcome the occasional accident or lapse of memory.

The collections need to be easily accessible to the pupils, and this emphasizes again the need for careful design of the resource islands. The collections need to be easily and quickly checkable at the end of lessons. Regular monitors can do this well, but the system should be designed for *instant* checking, i.e., the gaps should be apparent for all to see.

Here are checklists of the permanent occupants of the resource islands.

The stationery bank

A4 ruled paper

A4 and A5 plain paper

Suitable graph paper

Tracing paper

Blotting paper

Coloured paper (e.g., sugar paper)

Scrap paper

The best storage for stationery is the shallow drawer cabinet made of metal or fibreboard, but these are expensive. Alternatives are shallow plastic trays which slide inside a cabinet or trolley, or cardboard library boxes in which the sheets of paper stand upright.

Writing instruments and drawing equipment

Pens

Pencils

Rubbers

Rulers

Drawing instruments (pairs of compasses, dividers, set-squares, protractors)

Scissors

Adhesive tape

Coloured pencils

Pencil sharpener

Masking tape (for temporarily holding paper when drawing or tracing)

These all present an intriguing storage problem. They should be easily accessible, easily checked, and capable of being easily removed to secure storage when necessary. A number of labelled tins or boxes of various sizes and shapes are a good solution, especially if they can be handled as one unit (by placing them on a tray, for example). Another good solution is the block of wood with suitable holes in which the instruments stand upright. It is worth spending time experimenting with this item of storage; an accessible, self-checking arrangement can save a lot of time and a lot of fuss.

Reference books The classroom should contain a collection of subject reference books. Some of these should be on temporary loan from the

school library or the local authority's library's service. In addition every classroom should have these general reference books:
- a number of dictionaries suitable for the age-group;
- a single copy of a more advanced dictionary;
- a single volume encyclopedia, organized alphabetically.

Audio-visual hardware
Audio-cassette players
Small short-throw filmstrip/slide projectors
Filmstrip/slide viewers
These are the audio-visual aids most likely to be used by individual pupils or small groups of pupils. They are not intended for the teacher's use during class teaching. The audio-cassette player (*not a recorder*) is a cheap and versatile piece of equipment which deserves much wider use. Models available have two useful facilities: they can be battery or mains operated and they have output for headphones, so they can be used anywhere in the classroom. Batteries, however, can prove costly when the players are used heavily, therefore the mains operation should be used wherever possible. And they can be used without disturbing other pupils by:
- one pupil (using a single pair of headphones);
- two pupils (using two pairs of headphones with a special Y-piece);
- a small group (using a commercially-made distribution box).
Of course, these little machines cannot be used for making recordings. So if pupils' own recordings are required a small portable recorder will be necessary.

The short-throw filmstrip/slide projectors and viewers can also be bought fairly cheaply. But they are a bit trickier to operate than the cassette player, and most need a mains socket outlet. It is not worth purchasing special screens for individual and small-group viewing: a large cardboard box with a sheet of white drawing paper fixed inside will give quite good results in daylight. The provision of a mains cable right round the room, just above the height of the study booth screens, is ideal and can make an important contribution to the smooth running of the lessons.

Storage of resources

Printed resources
The best storage unit is an island bookshelf not more than 1.2 metres high. Cardboard or plastic library boxes are used to organize these

resources. It is useful to bind several together so that the system
and the whole collection can be moved together when require.

Audio-visual aids

If a large number of cassettes is required the best storage is either a
shallow shelf of just the right dimensions, so that the cassettes stand
upright, or a number of small boxes. Filmstrips in their cases are best
stored in small boxes. There are special storage units made to hold these
items firmly so that they can be individually labelled, but they tend to be
expensive.

Task card collection

These are usually A5 cards or standard file cards (203 × 127 mm). Plastic
'trial set' boxes with tabbed guide cards can be purchased from
stationers. A simple cardboard box of the right size will serve just as well,
although it is worth buying the tabbed guide cards.

The teacher's resources

The teacher's main tasks in the classroom are:
- to present information and ideas to the whole class;
- to organize and guide individual and small-group work.

The documents and tools for the second of these tasks can be best
described in Chapter 9 along with the appropriate procedures and
techniques. So we shall concentrate now on the equipment needed to
support the teacher's own presentations. The main support comes from
equipment that helps to convey the message in vivid and appealing ways.
Visual aids are essential.

Teacher's visual aids

The chalkboard

We must start with the chalkboard, which, well used, can be a very
powerful medium. There should be a generous surface area, and whether
this is achieved by fitting roller boards or simply using a large amount of
wall space seems to matter little. It is worth while to practise blackboard
techniques, for example, the intelligent and generous use of space; the
use of coloured chalks; the use of simple and bold graphics which clarify
concepts rather than attempt to describe detail.

Projected visuals

Nowadays it is fairly common for the blackboard to be supplemented by
projected visuals, which can be much more varied and effective. The first

requirement is a screen, standards for which have been suggested by the National Committee for Audio-Visual Aids in Education:

- screen width not less than one-sixth of the distance from screen to the rearmost viewing position;
- screen to be at least 1.2 m above floor level;
- position so that screen is angled against the main source of natural light;
- no student should have to view the screen at an angle much greater than 40° from the centre line;
- the screen must be able to be tilted for use with an overhead projector.

The second requirement is for a flexible control of both natural and artificial light. Perfect blackout is very difficult to obtain, and is not really required in normal use. Lined curtains are probably the best solution for shutting out the natural light, and can be made even more effective if a pelmet is fitted all round to prevent light creeping in at the edges. The teacher should experiment with different amounts of light under different conditions. It is often possible to dim the classroom just the right amount so that the pupils can read or write while having the benefit of clear images on the screen.

The third requirement is the projection equipment itself. The ideal provision would be:

- at the back of the room: a film projector and a filmstrip/slide projector;
- at the front of the room: an overhead projector, a television with video recorder, and a radio and/or tape recorder.

This means socket outlets are required at the front and back of the room, and also a television aerial connection. It would be unusual to see any classroom provided with all of this on a permanent basis. The best plan is to get the services right first, that is, the mains sockets, the aerial connections, and the screen, so that equipment borrowed from central resources can be properly used. After that, the priorities depend very much on subject and style of teaching.

Overhead projector

A good case can be made for the overhead projector. It has some formidable recommendations:

- it can provide a very large image in a good range of colours;
- material (e.g., text, maps, diagrams) can be prepared in advance, for display at the best moment of time from the learning point of view;
- sophisticated techniques can be used, to reveal parts of the image progressively, or to build up the image through the use of overlays;

- it can be used in an *ad hoc* way by the teacher to help in the explanation or elaboration of difficult points (just like a blackboard);
- throughout, the teacher remains firmly in control through facing the class, able to add to the image or to point things out without moving or turning.

Filmstrip/slide projector

The filmstrip/slide projector is another aid with strong claims:
- it is easy and quick to set up and operate;
- the quality of the projected image is very high, particularly of coloured photographs and coloured art work;
- there is a wide range of good quality software (slides and filmstrips) available commercially;
- the teacher who is a photographer can easily produce slides to meet particular needs.

Radio and television

With the valuable concessions relating to recording for educational purposes, radio and television are powerful additions to the teacher's armoury. Extra attention must be given to the robustness and stability of these pieces of equipment, and so it is better that they should be obtained from firms who specialize in the educational market. Exactly how these aids can be integrated into the teaching programme will be discussed in Chapter 6.

Information

Finally, whenever buying decisions have to be made about audio-visual hardware, the following authoritative sources of information and advice should be consulted:

1. The equipment catalogue of the Educational Foundation for Visual Aids. Published annually in July. Available from National Audio Visual Aids Centre, 254, Belsize Park, London, NW6 4BT.
2. Reprints of Technical Reports from the periodical *Visual Education*. Available from the National Audio Visual Aids Centre.
3. 'USPECS'. These are user specifications, prepared by users for the guidance of manufacturers. They are useful to *purchasers* too; they tell you what questions to ask! Available from Council for Educational Technology, 3, Devonshire Street, London, W1N 2BA.
4. Advice can be obtained from the experimental unit at the National Audio Visual Aids Centre and the regional centres of the Educational Foundation for Visual Aids in Bristol, Leeds, and Preston.

Summary

1. The classroom must serve for teacher presentations, for small-group work, and for individual study. It must provide ample work space for the pupils, and in order to do this it may be necessary to remove from the classroom all storage other than for the resources in current use.
2. A peripheral distribution of the pupils will create generous work space, good conditions for individual learning, flexible arrangements for small-group work, and a good layout for whole-class teaching. The resources can then occupy a central position with easy access for the pupils.
3. Versatile study booths can be easily made by simple adaptation.
4. The resource islands in the centre of the room should be purpose-designed for stationery; writing and drawing tools; reference books; audio-visual hardware; the main learning resources; the guidance materials (task cards); the assessment tests.
5. The teacher's resources would ideally consist of overhead projector, filmstrip/slide projector, film projector, TV/video-tape recorder, radio/audio-tape recorder, supported by a suitable screen and flexible light control.

6. Teacher presentation

This chapter is about class teaching, still the most common style of teaching in our classrooms. It is the layman's image of 'teaching'. Its main characteristic is its focus on the teacher as the organizer, the information giver, the discussion leader, the centre of attention. The class is relatively passive: listening, obeying instructions, responding to questions. Good teachers can play many variations on this theme and this chapter is devoted to the description and analysis of these variations.

Sadly, a lot of class teaching is dull and stifling, and there has been much criticism. The critics claim that class teaching relies too much on teacher talk, that the pupils are not active in their own learning, that individual differences are ignored, that pupils are regimented in such a way as to create low motivation, poor performance, and unsatisfactory teacher–pupil relationships. All this is true of class teaching at its worst, and when it is used as an exclusive method. No teacher, however dedicated, can be inspiring and stimulating for six hours a day and 200 days a year. So class teaching must take a modest place as one method and style amidst a larger repertoire. Less class teaching should lead to better class teaching. *Good* class teaching is a vital part of a teacher's repertoire; its strengths and its potential are considerable.

The personal attributes of the 'good' teacher

Many people, and this includes many teachers, believe that good teachers are born not made. There is a feeling that success in teaching depends almost entirely on 'personality' or 'charisma', and that technique and organization should spring spontaneously and intuitively from the personal attributes. Failures in teaching are due to fundamental personality defects and little can be done to remedy them. This is a dispiriting philosophy: in some teachers it can lead to an overbearing complacency; and in others, less fortunate, to a sense of hopelessness and defeat. It is a philosophy that the profession should reject. Teaching is a highly skilled activity which should and can be improved through systematic study, experiment, and practice.

It would be wrong, however, to ignore totally the personal attributes of the teacher. What is it about the teacher himself which makes him into a 'good' teacher? Why are some teachers regarded as 'bad' teachers? The man in the street is certain that he knows the answers. Yet the more people you ask the longer your list of desirable and undesirable qualities becomes. It begins to look something like this.

The 'good' teacher:

- knows his subject;
- can illustrate and apply his knowledge;
- expresses himself clearly;
- has good organizing ability;
- can control his pupils;
- is fair and impartial;
- is patient;
- is cheerful;
- is adaptable;
- is imaginative and stimulating;
- is sympathetic and a good listener;
- recognizes and praises achievement;
- is committed to the intellectual achievement of his pupils;
- is economical and relevant in verbal instructions and explanations.

The 'bad' teacher:

- has poor subject knowledge;
- has a limited repertoire of illustration and application;
- expresses himself in a confused manner;
- is slack in organization;
- has poor control of his pupils;
- is inconsistent and often biased;
- is intolerant;
- is inclined to be irritable;
- is unwilling to adapt;
- is dull and boring;
- is unsympathetic and bossy;
- focuses on mistakes and failures;
- puts administrative convenience and tidiness before the intellectual;
- is garrulous.

But these lists do not help us to establish priorities. Which of the 'good' attributes are absolutely critical and vital? If we insisted that *all* are essential, very few of us would be classified as 'good' teachers. Good teachers can develop from very diverse personalities.

A wise teacher knows his own personal strengths and weaknesses. He focuses on his strengths, and builds on them, because in improving one aspect of his style, the easier it becomes to improve other aspects. Likewise, in his dealing with colleagues, he focuses on their strengths, rather than on their weaknesses. Preoccupation with weaknesses can be counter-productive. Let us accept that some of the richness of the school experience may derive from the variety of personal styles that exist within a successful teaching force. Nevertheless, these lists can serve as useful checklists, acting as a reminder, and as a basis for personal objectives setting. Always be selective: choose one or two headings for personal improvement and try over a period of a few weeks to bring about the desired changes. The help of a friendly colleague is invaluable, since an independent observer can often perceive more accurately and can serve as confidant and counsellor. But avoid, at all costs, becoming too introspective, so that relationships in the classroom become forced and unnatural. Remember the countless teachers who have some odd quirks of character, whom their pupils remember with affection and respect. Rather than spend time worrying about personal inadequacies, it is better to concentrate on *techniques*.

The technique of exposition

Exposition is the informing, describing, and explaining which is part of every teacher's stock in trade. It is the school equivalent of the college lecture, but differs from that by its informality and its spontaneity. Few teachers would expect to get away with delivering a formal and contrived lecture to a class of school pupils. Instead the emphasis is always on variety of approaches and on pupil participation. Each will be analysed separately, and then possible syntheses examined.

Exposition itself is an attractive and powerful technique. Its purposes can be summarized as follows:
● to motivate and inspire pupils;
● to stimulate intellectual curiosity;
● to provide an 'advance organizer' of new subject matter;
● to provide a logical framework for a course of study;
● to review and consolidate;
● to give a personal account based on first-hand knowledge, or to give a personal interpretation of subject matter;
● to give a special emphasis to part of the work.
Exposition can take place at any time during a course of study but it is particularly valuable at the beginning, at the end, and at critical points such as topic changes or where the concepts are difficult.

The structure of class exposition

If the exposition has a clear structure that is apparent to the pupils it will be more likely to succeed in its purposes. Giving them an advance view of the territory to be covered, or the thought processes that will be used, are the most common ways of doing this. It helps to consolidate this if the pupils are given a handout which displays the structure of the exposition and requires some pupil contribution in order to complete it.

An alternative is to get the pupils to copy the framework from the blackboard. A few examples of such structures are given below.

The chronological/sequential structure

This is used where the teacher is explaining a sequence of events, or steps in a process, or a chain of causes and effects. The pupils' handout would simply have main headings and the teacher would pause to allow a few notes or key words to be entered by the pupils at the end of each stage. Alternatively, the handout could be a diagram in skeleton form which the pupil completes and makes his own during the exposition.

The deductive structure

In this the teacher explains and justifies a set of rules or principles and then goes on to describe a number of examples which illustrate the rules or principles. The emphasis is on the logical sequence of the thinking. When it is presented lucidly and vividly this structure can be stimulating, particularly with older pupils who are beginning to experience the satisfactions of abstract thinking. Some kind of diagram or set of structured notes is an essential aid, and is particularly valuable when pupils are given the opportunity to make their own contributions.

The inductive structure

In this the teacher presents a number of examples or case studies and helps the pupils to arrive at generalizations based on them. The lesson might have the following stages:
- first example described and discussed;
- second example described and discussed;
- similarities and differences noted;
- third example described and discussed;
- conclusions developed and justified;
- principles, rules, or generalizations established.

The problem-solving structure

This is an exciting approach and one to be commended. The lesson might have the following stages:
1. The problem is stated in as clear a manner as possible, using language appropriate to the age and experience of the pupils.
2. A first hypothesized solution is presented with arguments for and against being thoroughly explored.

3. A negative conclusion is reached and the problem is re-stated.
4. A second hypothesized solution is presented and the arguments are again thoroughly explored.
5. A negative conclusion is reached and the problem is re-stated.
6. A final solution is proposed, thoroughly criticized and tested, before being finally adopted as the best available solution given the present state of knowledge.

The approach can be highly motivating. If frequent use is made of rhetorical questions the pupils eagerly follow the development of the argument and are stimulated into using the imagination to try to anticipate the argument.

The 'compare and contrast' structure

This is a well-tried approach in which the pupils can become very involved in identifying similarities and differences between two sets of events, situations, or conditions. The material should be presented vividly and the use of structured notes regarded as an essential element in the lesson.

The subject heading structure

In the presentation of some topics pupils need to be given a lot of information. This can easily lead to dull teaching and so every effort should be made to make the material attractive and to keep the pupils involved. If it is done well this can be an effective way of providing the 'advance organizer' for a course of study.

The manner of the exposition

This is a matter of personal style and much of the technique of a good teacher is intuitive. However, it will benefit from analysis, and the following pieces of advice are offered on the understanding that they are not to be treated as rigid prescriptions for all people in all places at all times!

Get the attention of the class *before* you start

This can be done by a mixture of plain insistence and by *giving them something to do*. The latter may be little more than writing a title or an introductory statement, but it can help enormously to bring the class into the work frame of mind.

77

Your first few sentences must be attention holding

It is vital to appeal to their curiosity, or to surprise or intrigue them, or to move them emotionally. This must be done with great sensitivity of course. Too much of anything will be counter-productive. Take it seriously and quietly. Do not overdo it.

Keep your voice level to the minimum necessary

A low voice level creates a feeling of expectancy, gives a sense of importance to the occasion, and creates a mood of mutual confidence. Many teachers, accustomed only to the styles of traditional class teaching, are too noisy. They hector their classes, even when they are not quarrelling with them: a noisy teacher makes a noisy class! The message, therefore, is to create a quiet, serious, and trusting atmosphere.

Vary the volume and the pace to give variety

A low voice level provides an excellent base on which to build some variations. To excite and stimulate the pupils, a different pace or a different volume is required. When pupils are concentrating well on the words of the teacher, a line of reasoning can be made more exciting by the increased pace of delivery; the pupil gets the feeling of rapid mastery of new knowledge and a sense of exciting adventure in being able to stay with the argument. On other occasions an appeal can be made to feelings, by a more theatrical use of language. Education is just as much about feelings as about thinking, and we should not be ashamed to express our own feelings. But these projections of the teacher's 'personality' need to be tempered with sensitivity. Beware of over-indulgence, insincerity, and self-centred histrionics. They can easily develop into 'The Prime of Miss Jean Brodie'! Then there is the value and virtue of silence: the 'pregnant pause' is part of the theatrical technique, and used sparingly it can be effective. But, apart from that, pupils do need, during an exposition, moments to examine illustrations, to reflect on weighty statements or significant problems, and to consider their own responses. The teacher should encourage those silent interludes by identifying them and by suggesting to the pupils how to use them.

Make sure that the pupils never lose sight of the overall structure of the exposition

This principle is often summed up as follows: 'Tell them what you are going to say. Say it. Then tell them what you have said'. The principle is that of reinforcement. There is firm research evidence that pupils who have the structure of the lesson thoroughly explained to them tend to achieve better results.

Take great care in the use of language

Because teachers have been brought up in an academic tradition, making heavy use of reading and writing, they often fail to use the spoken word effectively. Their words are more appropriate for an academic textbook than for speaking to a group of young people. One often hears expressions like: 'A major feature of . . .'; 'An important factor in the development . . .'; and words such as: 'fundamental', 'incorporate', 'primarily', 'principal'. These can be obstacles to lucid exposition, if used thoughtlessly and to excess. It is better to choose:

- the concrete noun rather than the abstract;
- the active voice rather than the passive;
- the short sentence rather than the long;
- the simple sentence rather than the compound;
- the direct statement rather than the circumlocution;
- people as the subject wherever possible.

To introduce an abstract concept it is best to provide plenty of concrete examples, *which are within the experience of the pupils*, in order to provide temporary props for the new concept. Of course, it would be wrong to oversimplify language for the learner. The aim should be to gradually stretch the pupils' capabilities by the introduction of new vocabulary and by the occasional use of more complex statements.

Remember that much communication between teacher and pupil is non-verbal

How you look, where and how you stand, how you move are all observed and registered by the pupils. Distracting habits need to be eliminated, and confident teachers systematically find out what these are by, for example, asking the pupils or relying on the observations of a friendly colleague. Some gestures of course can be helpful, and can ensure greater concentration and more sympathetic responses. As always, overplaying the techniques can be counter-productive.

It is worth developing the skill of non-verbal communication to accomplish many of the small 'housekeeping' tasks of the classroom. This saves the use of language for the important communications about the content and ideas of the lesson. Communication by example, by signal, by gesture should all be practised.

The use of audio-visual aids

Exposition benefits enormously from the use of audio-visual aids. The use can vary from heavy dependence on the medium for the structure and content of the lesson (as in an educational broadcast) to the lightest use of a blackboard to illustrate a concept.

The blackboard

This is still the most common visual aid and, in capable hands, it can be very effective. Here are a few guidelines.

- Cleanliness is important. Have the board washed occasionally and keep the blackboard cleaners free of chalk dust.
- Make use of a wide range of coloured chalks.
- Do not spend long periods at the blackboard during the lesson. If detailed maps, diagrams or notes are required they should either be produced before the lesson, or built up bit by bit at intervals during the lesson.
- Use the blackboard as a *visual* aid to thinking, rather than as a substitute for the printed page. Information, ideas, and arguments can often be presented diagrammatically.
- Always prefer the bold and simple to the fine and detailed.
- Allocate a special area for important words (new vocabulary or difficult spelling). *Print* these words, using lower case rather than upper case letters.
- Get into the habit of thinking about the layout of the whole board. Long boards should not encourage equally long lines. Use generous margins at the top, bottom, and sides and generous spaces between items in order to help establish their separate identity.
- Be consistent: pupils are helped by the teacher who adopts conventions in layout, in the use of coloured chalks, in the use of underlining and boxing, and in the styles of lettering.

The overhead projector

The overhead projector has tended to replace the blackboard in lecturing in the adult world, mainly because transparencies can be carefully prepared in advance, stored, and easily transported to the site of the next lecture. It has not become so well-established in schools partly because of cost, but also because its advantages over the blackboard are not so great for the teacher who is permanently based on one site. Nevertheless there are major advantages which make the overhead projector preferable to the blackboard, for example, the potentially high quality of prepared transparencies; the very large screen size which can be used; the fact that the teacher operates *facing* the class. Here are guidelines for the use of the overhead projector.

- Regular cleaning is essential: dust causes a dirty, unsightly image.
- Prepared transparencies should be clear and bold and not cluttered with too much detail.
- The height of lettering needs to be watched: normally 8 mm should be regarded as the minimum height for capital letters.
- The teacher is often the main obstacle to the pupils' view of the screen! So when the teacher prefers to stand, the screen must be high and angled appropriately. An alternative is for the teacher to sit, with the transparency at desk-top height, by placing the projector on a chair or low stand.
- Always face the class and point to the transparency *not* to the screen.
- Have the class as close as possible, in order to create an intimate but business-like atmosphere.
- Use the projector as a visual aid to thinking rather than as a substitute for the printed page.
- Give careful consideration to design, e.g., generous margins and appropriate spacing.
- If you use sophisticated techniques like overlays or masking, make sure that you are proficient in handling the materials.
- Make sure that what you are showing on the screen and what you are saying are mutually supportive; switch off when the transparency has done its job.

The filmstrip/slide projector

This is a powerful aid to good exposition, and the software is relatively cheap. It is excellent for the projection of colour photographs and line drawings and there is a good chance of material which is both technically and educationally very acceptable. Here are basic guidelines for the use of the filmstrip/slide projector.

- The positioning of projector and screen needs careful planning. If permanent positioning is not possible then permanent marks should be made to ensure speedy and accurate positioning. The use of one screen for both overhead projector and filmstrip/slide projector may necessitate some compromise; alternatively use separate screens.

- Careful preparation is essential by viewing the frames and studying the teacher's notes.

- A quick scamper through a large number of frames is not usually the best use of the material. Each frame should be thought of as a rich source of information, ideas, or speculation. It may be that only three or four frames will be used in a lesson.

- Ideally the medium is best in a partial black-out but this creates problems for pupils' reading and writing, and any solution is bound to require compromise. It is important to establish a consistent way of operating.

Other media

Other media which can help to support a teacher's exposition are listed below.

Printed handouts	Audio recordings (tape or disc)
Photographic prints	Video recordings (tape or disc)
Real objects	Films
Models	Film loops
Live radio	Computer-based learning
Live TV	Game and simulation materials

Most teachers are forced to choose on the basis of the hardware and software that they have available. Where a choice does exist it is important to be systematic. This means looking critically again at the educational objectives, the content, and the needs of the pupils. Readers who are interested in the theoretical aspects of such decisions should consult Romiszowski (1981).

Techniques of questioning

Pure exposition is not normally regarded as a technique for lengthy periods in the classroom. Teachers know that the span of attention of school pupils has strict limits, and they emphasize a variety of approaches, and a lot of pupil participation. The most common technique for involving the pupils is the asking of questions. At its best it can stimulate and produce high-level thinking; at its worst it can be pedestrian and stifling.

Preparation

Although questioning is an interactive form of learning, it requires careful preparation. The teacher needs to have a mental picture of the build-up of knowledge or argument he wishes to achieve. This build-up starts with the familiar, with concrete examples, with simple concepts and gradually moves to the unfamiliar, to abstract ideas and to more advanced concepts. It is the lack of prior thought which leads to opening questions like: 'This lesson is about the Boer War. Who can tell me what they know about the Boer War?' The teacher might be lucky and get an interesting response to work on, but careful planning and a phased introduction of the topic is likely to produce better results.

Phases of a questioning session

The planned phases of a questioning session might look something like this.

Phase 1: stimulus The teacher presents a picture, a map, a drawing, a piece of text, a short exposition, a sound, which rouses curiosity and starts the questioning.

Phase 2: development The teacher's questions help pupils build upon the existing knowledge and understanding.

Phase 3: generalization The teacher's questions provide situations so that pupils can transfer their new knowledge and understanding, and can recognize principles and rules.

Phase 4: performance and feedback The teacher's questions give pupils the opportunity to demonstrate their new understanding. They are tested on their knowledge and invited to apply it.

The questions themselves

Much of the technique of questioning, nevertheless, involves thinking on one's feet. The questions must be adapted to the responses of the pupils, and so the precise wording cannot be prepared in advance. There are a number of questioning skills which need to be developed.

The language must be simple, clear, and unambiguous

This point was elaborated in the section on exposition, and the same guidance can be applied to questioning.

The questioning should start with observation and identification

The key word is 'What?' Here are some examples.

'What are the people in this picture doing?'

'What is the difference between these two shapes?'

'What surprised you in this brief description?'

'What is this?'

The questioning should develop in a way that encourages pupils to talk in a constructive way

'What?', 'When?', and 'Where?' questions tend to get one word answers. 'Do you . . .?' and 'Don't you . . .?' questions tend to get 'Yes' or 'No'. Words and expressions likely to evoke fuller answers are:

'Why . . .?'

'How . . .?'

'What would happen if . . .?'

The questions should build up to higher levels of thinking

The 'How' and 'Why' questions may be classified as:

- using evidence to come to conclusions;
- applying rules and principles to specific instances;
- solving problems;
- using imagination;
- developing hypotheses to explain observations;
- evaluation.

The pupils' responses

Getting the best responses calls for patience and skill. There are a number of useful hints.

Be prepared to wait for an answer

If a question is greeted with initial silence there is a natural tendency to fill the gap. This leads to teacher dominance of the proceedings and pupils withdraw further into themselves. There must, of course, be a limit to the waiting time. Pupils usually signal their embarrassment, and that is the time to intervene. But, generally speaking, many teachers can improve their questioning techniques by being prepared to wait just a little longer!

Encourage participation

Praise the good answers. Use the names of those who participate. Preserve the self-esteem of those who give wrong answers by taking their answers seriously and by rewarding them with praise or a friendly gesture. Give help, if it appears to be needed, during an answer. A single word, a nod, a rephrasing will often encourage a pupil to press on. The skill is to know when to withdraw.

Try to involve all the pupils

The time-honoured practice is for the pupils to indicate their desire to respond by raising the hand. This has the disadvantage of focusing the questioning too much on the bright and eager at the expense of slower pupils. It also encourages the teacher to point to a number of pupils in rapid succession in search of the 'best' answer. It is good practice for the teacher frequently to ignore the raised hands in favour of involving someone else. A particularly reluctant pupil can be helped by being nominated to answer an easy question *before* the question is asked. Another danger to avoid in selecting pupils to answer questions is the tendency to have dealings with only a limited area of the classroom so that some pupils are seriously neglected. The front and the centre may get more than their fair share of attention!

Encourage the response which expresses the personal thoughts or feelings of the pupils

Learning to communicate in an authentic and responsible way is right at the heart of education.

Encourage the response which is bold and imaginative

Praise such a response, regardless of its correctness.

Encourage respect for the contribution of others

Teach the pupils, by example and precept, the skills of constructive criticism and courteous deliberation. Do not accept sarcasm, mockery, aggression and destructive criticism.

Discussion techniques

Effective questioning naturally leads into discussion. There is no clear boundary between the two. As soon as pupil–pupil interactions take place in addition to teacher–pupil interactions then the lesson has acquired some of the characteristics of a discussion. But it has to be conceded that the size of the average class is far in excess of the optimum size of a discussion group. So class discussion should be thought of as a variant of teacher questioning.

The teacher needs to be firmly in control. The objectives of the discussion should be clearly established and the rules of procedure laid down. It helps to rearrange seating so that pupils can see and hear each other easily.

Once the 'housekeeping' has been properly arranged, the teacher, in his role as discussion leader, needs to exercise a democratic rather than an authoritarian style. All the techniques of skilful questioning need to be brought to bear with the additional skill of withdrawal into neutrality. Pupil participation must be encouraged with reinforcement, prompting, and occasional summaries as to where the discussion has reached.

It is wise to set a strict time limit to a discussion and to bring it to a satisfactory close by summarizing the main points made and conclusions reached. Discussion techniques are particularly appropriate for objectives concerned with personal attitudes, and for those concerned with problem-solving.

Summary

1. Personal attributes do contribute to the making of a good teacher. A checklist is useful, but it is not wise to become too introspective. It is better to concentrate on techniques.
2. Good exposition requires a sound structure. Examples are:
   - chronological/sequential
   - deductive
   - inductive
   - problem-solving
   - compare/contrast
   - subject heading
3. Good exposition requires techniques:
   - get and hold attention
   - consider voice level
   - vary the volume and pace
   - emphasize the structure
   - take care in the use of language
   - use non-verbal communication
4. Audio-visual aids enrich exposition.
5. Questioning techniques involve:
   - careful preparation of the structure;
   - questions formulated for clarity, for pupils' observation, and to develop higher-order thinking;
   - pupils' responses.
6. Discussion techniques.

7. The management of individual and small-group learning

This chapter looks at the complex task of managing individual and small-group learning. 'The needs of the individual' are widely accepted as a legitimate source of inspiration and guidance in education. Many teachers believe that tailoring educational provision to the needs of the individual is a major aim. There is, however, much confused thinking and it may help to stipulate some definitions.

Individual learning—a comprehensive term for all learning where the emphasis is on the individual rather than on the group. It therefore includes situations where all the pupils in a class are engaged on a common task, but are working privately.

Individualized learning—a more specific term for the learning experiences which have been tailored to individual needs. Aspects of individualized learning include, 'working at your own pace', and resources and guidance materials that are individually presented.

Independent learning—a general term that focuses on the organization and decision-making aspects of learning. A learner in such a system enjoys a degree of freedom from the control of the teacher, making many of the decisions about content, work programme, and work styles for himself.

Resource-based learning—a similar concept to independent learning in that the pupil gets much of the data, stimuli, guidance, and organization from a rich collection of resources rather than from the teacher. However, substantial support from the teacher is not precluded. Much of the discussion about these systems of learning has focused on criticism of class teaching and claims that the alternatives will provide remedies. The polarized arguments are outlined in Table 7.1. This is probably an overstatement of the case. Good class teaching is an essential component in any teacher's repertoire. Nevertheless, there is still insufficient exploitation of the real benefits resulting from the more individualized and independent systems.

Table 7.1   *Arguments in favour of alternative systems of learning*

Class teaching systems	The alternative systems
Create a passive attitude in the pupils.	Offer a more active sort of learning.
Regiment the pupils, all doing the same thing at the same time.	Allow individual variations in content, pace, and style.
Encourage pupils to become dependent on the teacher.	Foster study skills and provide a preparation for life-long education.
Create a permanent confrontation between teacher and pupils.	Permit a 'workshop' atmosphere which establishes healthy teacher/pupil relationships.
Force students and young teachers to 'fly solo' at a very early stage.	Improve the induction of students and young teachers through contact with small groups and individuals.
Create inflexible school systems.	Offer possibilities of solutions to current problems such as falling rolls, uneconomic groups, staff shortages.

Good individual learning depends on:

1. A well-prepared course consisting of learning resources, pupil guidance, and teacher control materials.
2. A sound structure for the management of the classroom.
3. A well-designed set of operating procedures for classroom management.

The well-prepared course

The preparation of the study units for a course was described in Chapter 2. Each study unit includes:

- a boxed and numbered collection of resources;
- a set of task cards for individual and small-group use;
- a master plan giving instant information to the teacher about the task cards and resources.

These three items represent the key components in the operation of a system of individualized learning. Further details are now provided about these components in action in the classroom.

Differentiation

In an ideal world all the materials would be highly differentiated in order to meet the varied needs of all the individuals who would use the system. However, individual differences are extraordinarily complex, and, at the same time, individual pupils do not fit easily into simple categories. In the real world it simply is not possible to create the diversity of materials which could be used. So what is the teacher to do?

It is suggested that the following strategies should be used in order of importance.

1. Create as much time as possible for briefing and coaching in advance of the pupil's confrontation with the learning materials. The teacher's knowledge of a pupil's abilities, styles, personality, and problems can never be superceded by prepared written material, however good. So the teacher needs to develop the skills of diagnosis and tutoring. The task cards and, to a lesser extent, the resources should be regarded as raw material which needs *shaping* to individual needs. They can be expanded, contracted, modified, partly replaced by other materials, or even totally rejected in favour of an *ad hoc* prescription.

2. If the briefing and coaching are being done well, it may be possible to manage with as few as three task cards for each discrete activity. Aim to make them really different from each other. The first should be big and challenging, providing a lot of work for an able pupil. It should leave much of the organization and decision-making to the pupil, and it should involve higher levels of thinking, for example, analysis problem-solving, hypothesis formation. In addition, it should make use of resources outside the classroom. It should be the normal practice for the teacher to amend this by cutting it back to the individual pupil's capabilities and interests.

   The second task card should offer a carefully structured approach with lots of guidance to help the pupil reach some of the higher levels of thinking. There should be some limited opportunities for the pupil to organize some of the work in his own way.

   The third task card should give very careful but simple guidance so that the slower pupil will be able to accomplish the tasks easily. Some 'modelling' of the kind of response expected will help. It is assumed that even the slowest pupils will find such a card within their capabilities. The teacher's task will normally be to add to and enrich the tasks according to the individual pupil's interests and activities.

3. If the first two strategies have been successfully implemented it may be possible to leave the learning resources in their raw, un-differentiated state. Rewriting the resources at two or three different levels is a chore most teachers prefer not to have! Add-on techniques which can be helpful are:
   - marking significant passages;
   - making a recorded reading of a difficult text (easily and quickly done without editing).

But modification of the learning resources should assume a low priority compared with the other two strategies.

Extension and enrichment

Well before the teaching is due to start, the teacher should make comprehensive notes on the master plan about the nature and location of other resources suitable for enriching the study unit. This means investigating the school library and the local authority support services. It is vital that this is done thoroughly so that the pupils gain experience in finding and handling resources of all kinds, and are in no way restricted by the resources selected or created for the classroom.

Time management

Time is the most precious resource of all. The amount of time that each pupil actually spends *on task*, and the amount of time the teacher spends working with pupils *on their tasks*, are the two most powerful predictors of successful learning. So efforts spent in setting up automatic procedures and routines for handling the everyday 'housekeeping' of the classroom are well worth while. This includes the provision and checking of stationery, writing and drawing instruments, and audio-visual hardware. Every opportunity should be taken to give jobs to pupils. The possibility of getting help from students, parents, and ancillary staff should always be borne in mind.

Finally there is the computer. We do not need the expensive computer around which a whole system of learning is created, but rather the small, cheap model which can sit quietly in the corner of the classroom working non-stop on some routine tasks. These tasks might be:
- administering simple mastery tests and giving the pupil immediate feedback;
- providing practice in a straightforward component of the course.

Such services would generate new time for the teacher which could be used for the kind of tasks only a human being can do well. The programmes for the computer tasks are relatively simple to create, and the support from teachers wishing to do this is growing very rapidly.

The sound structure for the management of the classroom

Any organization which consists of more than two or three people has a structure of some kind, with its departments, sections or units, each of which has a membership, clear roles, and a set of external relationships.

Yet it is surprising how many teachers can think of a school class only as a single entity or as an amorphous collection of thirty individuals. Good management of individual and small-group learning demands an organizational structure.

The pair

This is an excellent unit for collaboration working. The partners can sit alongside each other giving mutual aid. Decisions can be quickly and easily made. The effort can all go on the task rather than on 'politics' and 'liaison'.

The small group

There is agreement among researchers that five is the optimum size for a small group. It has been observed that this is big enough to provide a reasonable variety of contributions to the jobs in hand; and it is small enough to guarantee that each member feels an obligation to participate, i.e., there is no tacit withdrawal. Also the odd number is thought to be an advantage, since the group must always produce a majority view on any decision instead of being locked into two intransigent camps. Unfortunately, when pupils are working in pairs some would find that their partnership would have to be broken when they were combining to form a small group of this size. For this reason a small-group size of four or six might be preferred. The small group is used for discussion, cooperative problem-solving, games and simulations.

The division

This is the largest unit within the class and it could consist of two small groups (eight or ten pupils). So there could be three or four divisions within the class. The division is a useful unit for the allocation of tasks and resources, where total individualization seems inappropriate. For example, many classes in the nine to thirteen age range are large, and pupils at this age need to have fairly frequent guidance from the teacher. A teacher who attempts total individualization for such a class puts a considerable strain on his own capacity to respond adequately to the rapid succession of pupils needing guidance. By virtue of some mental and physical agility the teacher might cope, but it is likely that thoughtful and reflective interchanges between teacher and pupil will be squeezed out. It is better to have all the pupils in one division working on the same topic. The advantages are that briefing and coaching of the whole division is a great economy in the use of the teacher's time, and the teacher is able to concentrate more on the limited range of subject-matter and so give better help and guidance. If the subject matter is not sequential (and rarely is it essential for it to be so) then the four divisions of the class can be organized as a rotating circus. The loss of individual briefing may seem to some to be a great sacrifice. In fact, the teacher chooses his position on a continuum. At one end the teacher can choose individual briefing with long periods of non-contact time for the pupils; and at the other end large-group briefing with much shorter periods of non-contact time between. Generally speaking, the former can work well with older and intellectually mature pupils while the latter seems more appropriate for the younger and intellectually immature pupils. A logical structure for the class which the pupils understand gives a sense of security, stability, and discipline. It is worth a little effort at the outset to get it clearly defined. One important decision is in the allocation of pupils to the various groupings. Friendship and personal preferences should count a great deal, but from the point of view of effective working the following principles seem sound:

- a pair of pupils should not be widely dissimilar in their attainments;
- a small group should tend to heterogeneity rather than to homogeneity.

It is worth adding that the heterogeneous small groups need not be the only grouping used in learning. The teacher can form an *ad hoc* group from the pupils of one division according to any criteria.

The operating procedures of classroom management

The transition from class teaching to individually prescribed learning

This needs to be handled carefully. The danger is that the pupils will suddenly all at once require resources, stationery, writing and drawing materials, and some decisions from the teacher. Chaos seems certain. The transition can be smoothly achieved by setting all pupils a common task to be tackled individually at the end of the class teaching phase. While this is being done the teacher can circulate the class, quietly allocating a task card to each pupil. Pupils will finish the common task at staggered times and so there will be less pressure on the resources stand and on the teacher. As soon as the teacher is satisfied that the operation is going smoothly, a first briefing session can be undertaken with one of the divisions.

The cycle of individual learning

Fig. 7.1 shows the study tour which the pupils follow several times during a phase of individual learning.

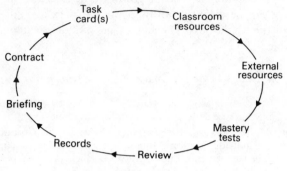

Fig. 7.1   *A 'study tour'*

The briefing

During individual learning the briefing is the most important responsibility undertaken by the teacher. Its quality has a direct influence on the quality of the pupils' work and on their subsequent knowledge and understanding. It is worth emphasizing this point because many enthusiasts for individual learning believe that the teacher's main function during this process is to help pupils when they get into difficulties. The conclusions of a six-year study funded by the American National Institute of Education are as follows:

> *Structuring the lesson and giving directions on task procedures were positively associated with high student success.*
> Teachers who gave directions more often and spent time discussing the structure of the lesson had students who showed a greater rate of high success. Anecdotal reports suggest that students sometimes do not know what they are supposed to be doing or how they are supposed to mark a particular worksheet. Clarifying activities by the teacher can help raise student achievement by affecting the high success rate component of Academic Learning Time.
> *Explanation specifically in response to student need is negatively associated with high student success.*
> One teaching behaviour was explanation in response to student need. This occurred when a student did not understand something and the teacher explained it to him. Most explanation-need occurred during seat-work. Students who received more explanation in response to need tended to have fewer high success tasks and more low success tasks. From a slightly different perspective, a student who had more need received more explanation in response to need. Apparently though, the explanation did not solve the problem since, in the long run, the student had little high

93

success. Frequent need for explanation may be a signal that changes are needed in the student's instructional program, either in the difficulty of the assignments or in preparation for seat-work.

The message is clear; the importance of advance briefing is paramount.

What is the optimum size of the groups to be briefed? Theoretically the briefing can be aimed at an individual, a pair, a small group, a division, or the whole class. The advantages and disadvantages are set out in Table 7.2.

Table 7.2 *Advantages and disadvantages of altering group size*

	Advantages	Disadvantages
Reducing the size of the group	More intimate. Better prospects for individualization. More detailed agreements. Pupils' grasp of the guidance easily checked.	Meagre time allocation. Pupils spend less time in contact with teacher. Longer periods between briefings.
Increasing the size of the group	More time. Explanations can be developed. Shorter time between briefings.	More difficult to individualize the guidance. Less intimate. Checking of pupils' understanding more difficult.

Decisions about the size of groups for briefing can vary according to class size, age of the pupils, their intellectual maturity, and the content of the subject matter. There is no reason why the size of groups cannot be varied on different occasions with the same class. Let us consider a typical briefing for a division of a class. It can take place anywhere in the classroom but pupils should be seated as close to the teacher as possible. Each pupil should have the necessary task cards and resources. An agenda might look like this:

● the teacher explains and clarifies the objectives of the tasks to be performed;

● the teacher gives general guidance, at the simplest level, about what is to be done and how it is to be done;

● the teacher gives specific guidance to individual pupils, or to appropriate groupings of individuals, with the aim of modifying the printed instructions to suit individual needs;

● pupils are asked, in turn, to recite their specific instructions and to ask any questions;

● the teacher sets a time scale for the individual work.

When the briefing is concluded the teacher updates the records of the individual members of the division.

The study tour

As soon as the briefing is finished the pupils collect any further materials that they require and return to their bases to start work. During this phase pupils should be free to collect any additional material they may require without asking permission. They should also be free to consult other pupils within the division. Emphasis is now being placed on their independence.

If mastery tests have been included in the task instructions pupils should be allowed to administer these themselves and to check the results themselves. These tests are for reinforcement and for feedback to the pupils. They are not part of the teacher's assessment, and so high standards of accuracy are not so important. What is important is that the teacher is free to concentrate on the truly creative aspects of the work.

The review

When a pupil has completed his tasks the work needs to be reviewed. The teacher may attempt to do this during class time, but this can easily dominate the teacher's time to such an extent that time for prior briefing becomes difficult to find. Reluctantly the teacher is likely to conclude that marking must be done outside class time. It is useful to spread the load by taking in at the end of the lesson *only* completed tasks. At the beginning of the next lesson the small number of pupils whose work has been marked should do any necessary corrections and then report for the review. This, of necessity, must be brief, and should indicate the teacher's view of the strengths and weaknesses of the completed work.

A further problem now emerges. Members of a division are not likely to complete a cycle of tasks at exactly the same time. What about the early finishers?

Arrangements for occupying waiting time

Something needs to be available to the early finishers so that the waiting time can be profitably used. A short list of practical suggestions, from artwork to lists for reading, viewing and listening, is provided below.

Activities   Artwork relevant to the topic (e.g., book or folder covers, wall displays).
Analysis of personal records (see next section on records).
Mini-research topics using class library references.
Reading—class library reference material.
Viewing slide collections or listening to tapes.

Communicating the ideas to pupils A bold poster bearing a caption such as: 'What to do with those spare moments'.

Special task cards for mini-research topics.

Lists for reading, viewing, and listening.

The main essential is that the problem should be thoroughly examined during the preparation stage and the arrangements clearly explained to the pupils, so that 'Please sir, what can I do now?' is not heard in the classroom.

The pupils' records

Much of the effectiveness of individual learning depends on the kinds of records that the teacher is able to keep. In fact, it is almost impossible to carry out good briefing and review without good records. This is the information the teacher needs about each pupil:

- What tasks has he already completed?
- What strengths and what weaknesses have been apparent in those completed tasks?
- What is he engaged on now?
- What contractual obligations has he made for the present task?
- What marks or grades has the teacher awarded?

The pupil ought to have some record too. Is it possible for teachers to keep detailed records of this kind without running into serious problems of time management? If we are going to succeed, the system must be simple and elegant. And it needs to be tied in with the system of marking adopted by the teacher. The description that follows is one teacher's solution to these problems. Readers may not accept all the assumptions, and they may find that their own teaching needs somewhat different approaches. Nevertheless, the description may help to illustrate the search for simplicity and elegance.

Recording and marking: a linked system

The system must operate at two levels:

- the technical competencies: language, presentation and content;
- the educational objectives for which the course has been designed.

Marking and records must serve both these levels. The marking system uses a coding system to indicate technical flaws in the work.

Table 7.3 *Coding system for marking and records*

Language	Presentation	Content
S = Spelling	H = Handwriting	A = Inaccurate
W = Wrong word	L = Layout of the page	E = Inadequately explained
C = Capital letter	T = Titles or labels	D = Insufficient detail
P = Punctuation	Hd = Headings	R = Faulty reasoning

Success in achieving educational objectives is marked by the award of a credit (represented by a gold star in this particular system) with a code number alongside to indicate which of the objectives is being referred to. A simple coding system might look like this:

1 = Good knowledge demonstrated.

2 = Understanding of important concepts demonstrated.

3 = Research skills have been applied.

4 = Information has been presented lucidly (in written or graphic form).

5 = Information has been interpreted well.

6 = Critical thinking has been demonstrated.

7 = The work suggests the development of sincere attitudes and values.

Of course the use of the two coding schemes does not prevent the teacher writing comments at length about a pupil's work.

The pupil as record-keeper

When the marked work is returned, the pupil takes over. Pupils are generally good at record keeping, especially if they are provided with a business-like form and a clear set of instructions. This system provides them with an A4 sheet which can be kept in a ring binder or pasted inside an exercise book. Fig. 7.2 shows the design and the conventions used. The pupil's record thus gives a useful summary of strengths and weaknesses. It provides the raw material for a profile of achievement, which is a more accurate and detailed statement than a single mark. It is quite feasible for a pupil's work which is badly presented and littered with spelling mistakes to receive credits for the quality of thought behind it!

The teacher's mark book

When the pupil comes to the teacher for his review, the teacher can take the opportunity to update his own record. The conventional mark book does not provide enough space for detailed records, but a great deal can be accomplished by allotting a double page of a mark book to a single

Debits

	Language				Presentation				Content				Task card	Credits Objectives						
	S	W	C	P	H	L	T	Hd	A	E	D	R		1	2	3	4	5	6	7
	•••••	•	•				••			•••	••		①	*		*				
	•••		••	•			•	•	•	•	••		④			**		*		
													2							
													3							
													5	*	*	*	*	*	*	*

Key to debits

S = Spelling
W = Wrong word
C = Capital letters
D =

Key to credits

1. Good knowledge demonstrated
2. Understanding of important concepts demonstrated
3. Research skills have been applied
4.

Fig. 7.2 *Design of a pupil's own record*

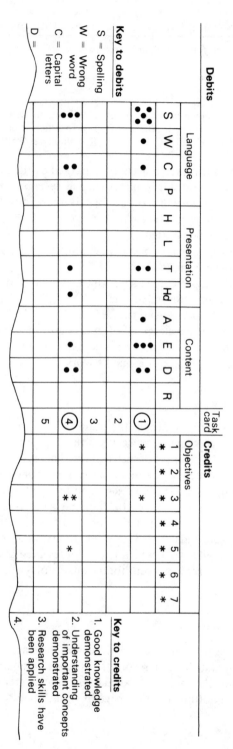

division. The layout of such a page is shown in Fig. 7.3. Note that the pupils are listed in their work groupings, not alphabetically. The teacher has a lot to pack into the small boxes and it is necessary to devise one's own shorthand. A useful convention is to use the upper half of the box

Division A

Group 1				Task card
John Smith	Alan Jones	Mary Keen	Ann Harris	
S.E.		2.5 A		1
	Omit 4. Drawing H.L.			2
				3
Lib. SI. 3		Lib. SI. Brown 3.5 A	I	4
	H.L. H 2			5
				6

Fig. 7.3 *A design for a teacher's mark book. Division A occupies a double-page spread. Group 1 on the left, group 2 on the right*

for notes made at the briefing, and the lower half for notes made at the review. In the example, John Smith did task card 1 and the teacher recorded that spelling needed attention and some explanations were inadequate. At the next briefing John was advised to go beyond the task card by exploring the subject index in the main library. At review the teacher expressed satisfaction with the research that John had done. Lines can be used to record results of conventional attainment tests, or examination results, and if a normal grade is required for each task, this can be incorporated within the boxes.

The management of the teacher's time

How can the teacher fit in all the briefing, reviewing, record keeping, class teaching, group tutoring, and supervision? It is useful to start from a mental picture of the 'ideal' lesson. The sequence of events might look something like this:

- Supervise the arrival of the class and the start of work.
- Tour of the room to check all on task and to pick up any 'quickies' (questions about detail, answered quickly).
- Call pupils in turn who have work for review.
- Another supervisory tour.
- Call a division which is ready for next briefing.
- Another supervisory tour.

- Call a division which is ready for next briefing.
- A supervisory tour. Give help to individuals or small groups on an *ad hoc* basis.
- Supervise the packing up.

Of course, flexibility is also important, particularly in the case of the supervisory tours which may have to be extended if there are a number of difficulties cropping up. On the other hand, when things are going smoothly it is worth while extending the briefing or doing more small-group coaching.

The main objective in time management is to create more time for *teaching*, i.e., presenting information and ideas to the pupils, advising them about the organization of their work, monitoring their work, and giving them feedback on their performance. As much as possible the following should be eliminated: too many 'quickies', too many discipline confrontations, 'housekeeping' duties, administration.

Improving time problems

The teacher who constantly feels pressed for time should make a conscious effort to improve matters. Some practical suggestions are outlined below.

1. Identify tasks which are totally unnecessary and get rid of them. Ask the question: 'What would happen if this were not done at all?' If in doubt *try* doing without it. It can be easily reinstated if it proves to be really necessary.
2. Delegate jobs to the pupils. Make sure they are well briefed. They need to have a clear vision of the results that you want.
3. Identify and deal with recurring crises. If the crisis has happened before, it might happen again. Can a routine be established which will deal with it smoothly or automatically?
4. Be brief in discussion of routine administration matters. Pupils can get accustomed to the teacher who says everything ten times!
5. If the need for briefing sessions seems to be very frequent, consider lengthening the size of tasks given on any one occasion. There is no need to be confined to *one* task card.
6. If 'quickies' proliferate, resolve to review the resources and the task cards (particularly the latter) with a view to eliminating ambiguities and overwhelming difficulties.
7. Be persistent. Time problems need to be reviewed frequently. There is always the danger of slipping back into bad habits.

Summary

1. There are substantial benefits to be gained from a use of individualized systems of learning.
2. Good preparation of learning resources, guidance for pupils, and control documents for the teacher is an essential prerequisite. Important considerations are:
   - adequate provision for individual differences;
   - arrangements for enrichment and extension;
   - the planning of good time management.
3. A sound organizational structure is necessary. The roles of the pair, the small group, and the division need to be defined.
4. The operating procedures of classroom management must be deliberately planned. These include:
   - careful arrangements to effect the transition from class teaching to individual learning;
   - efficient briefing of groups of pupils by the teacher;
   - a short review of an individual pupil's work after the completion of a task;
   - explicit arrangements for those 'waiting' periods when a pupil is ready for a new briefing before the other members of his division.
5. A comprehensive system of records is an essential support for the management of individual learning. The participation of the pupils is essential.
6. The teacher needs to study the management of his own time, and to seek every opportunity to improve on it.

8. The techniques of individual learning

This chapter looks more closely at the processes involved in individual learning and at the teacher's repertoire of strategies and tactics for different 'types' of individuals.

Individual styles

It is useful to recognize that the pupils in any classroom will exhibit different styles in their approach to their work. In the acquisition of knowledge and understanding, some will rely heavily on written words and symbols; others will make more use of spoken language; others will have a natural response to maps, diagrams, and similar forms of visual representation.

In their search for meaning, some will reach it through their sensitivity to the needs and feelings of people; others through a commitment to a set of values or an appreciation of beauty; others through their achievements in making something.

As the pupils mature intellectually different styles of reasoning will begin to emerge: comparing and contrasting; looking for cause–effect relationships; speculative thinking, deductive thinking. Pupils differ also in the way they react to the life and work of the classroom. Some constantly seek the attention of the teacher; others are inclined to be solitary; others seem to thrive on collaboration with fellow pupils.

What should the teacher do about pupils' personal styles? Respect and encourage the development of individual styles? Or try to guide each pupil to a more extended and well-balanced repertoire? The answer must surely be to do both: respect the individual's present preferences and encourage their development, while at the same time creating opportunities for the pupil to try out different ways of working.

Exceptional pupils

Every pupil is unique, but there are some individuals who differ so much from any idea of an average or norm that they must be regarded as exceptional. For such pupils an adaptation of the regular classroom arrangement must be regarded as necessary in order that they may maximize their full potential. Pupils may be regarded as exceptional for reasons of physical handicap, mental handicap, emotional disturbance, or for reasons of very high general ability or specific giftedness. Whatever the reasons for them being regarded as exceptional there are two basic questions to be answered:

1. Should these exceptional pupils be given entirely separate educational provision, in special schools or special classes?
2. What are the precise adaptations appropriate for each group?

Mainstreaming

In the past the answer to the first question has been to segregate exceptional pupils from the mainstream of educational provision. This has meant the creation of special schools and special classes, and a hierarchical system of selection by ability at the secondary stage of education. In recent years the trend has been the other way, with the emphasis on integration within the mainstream of all pupils. The arguments from both sides seem equally convincing. On the one hand, it is argued that exceptional pupils left in regular classrooms tend to be rejected by their fellows and neglected by the teacher. On the other hand, it is argued that exceptional pupils in special classes are isolated from normal social experiences and may suffer a loss of self-esteem (in the case of the handicapped). The results of research has tended to reinforce these contradictory views. As a result the mainstreaming movement now tends to work on the principles outlined below:

1. Every child is entitled to an education in the *least restrictive educational* setting.
2. This should be assumed in the first place to be the normal classroom.
3. Where a normal classroom does not seem to be *wholly* appropriate for a pupil, then the child is moved from the mainstream only to the minimum extent which appears necessary. For some, this may well mean total removal but for most it will mean some kind of support arrangement, with special arrangements for part of the time.

The application of these principles in school organization means that a teacher can assume that, in any class, there will be a number of pupils for whom the normal educational programme needs to be adapted. We now need to consider two examples of these adaptations: slow learners and very able pupils.

Slow learners

This is a commonly used expression to refer to a group of pupils within a class, and yet the causes of their slow learning may vary considerably. Some may be mentally retarded, but not sufficiently for them to be placed full-time into special schools. Others may be slow learners because of behaviour disorders, or because of social or cultural handicaps, or their difficulties may be quite specific and of a temporary nature. Such pupils need studying carefully before any attempt is made to prescribe alternative educational treatment. It is worth while attempting to produce a detailed *written* description of each individual's problems. Table 8.1 provides a checklist of possible headings and subheadings.

Table 8.1 *Checklist for use in the study of individual slow learners*

Physical	*Social*
Size and weight	Relationships at home
Strength	Relationships with fellow pupils
General physical coordination	Relationships with teacher
Manual dexterity and coordination	Affection
Eyesight	Aggression
Hearing	
Speech	*School record*
	Performance in basic skills
Intellectual	Speed of work
Knowledge	Thoroughness of work
Experience	Efficiency in routines
Interests	Attendance and punctuality record
Language	
Language—vocabulary and sentences	
Reasoning	
Personality	
'Strength' of character	
Self-image	
Confidence	
Cooperativeness	
Stability	

Identification of slow learning pupils is the first step and the very act of trying to define the problem for each individual pupil is the first step in providing an adapted programme.

Lines of support outside the classroom
Outside help is, of course, vital to success. The first line of support can come from the school's own remedial department. The specialist staff

can add to the teacher's own informal diagnosis with a more systematic programme of testing, interviewing, diagnosis, and monitoring of progress. In many schools where a policy of mainstreaming is adopted members of the remedial department spend a lot of time working closely with the regular class teachers, recommending additional resources for slow learners, modifying task cards, and working inside the classrooms in order to give the slow learners more intensive help.

A second line of support comes from the various 'helping' agencies which cooperate with the school. These include the education welfare officers, the educational psychologists, the specialist teachers from various centres such as a Reading Centre or a Multicultural Education Centre, the social workers, and the nurses and doctors of the Schools' Health Service. The school should have well-established links with all of these, and the teacher who is really determined about slow learners will be familiar with the arrangements and eager to exploit them.

Help from the pupil's teacher: suggested techniques

Most of the help for the slow learner will come from the teacher in the classroom. Fortunately, the techniques are not markedly different from those that work well with all children. It is more a difference in degree rather than a difference in kind. Slow learners are most helped by teachers who are thoroughly aware of the individuals' backgrounds and problems, and who are prepared to apply intensive efforts to helping them overcome these problems. A number of practical suggestions follow.

Emphasize relationships

This must be the first priority. A warm, accepting and trusting relationship needs to be established *before* any consideration is given to the actual learning programme. It is important to start where the child is—in terms of emotions, knowledge, experience, and desires.

Make contact with the home

Contact should be made, not for the purpose of telling the parents what they should do, but in order to enhance the teacher's own awareness and understanding.

Spend more time giving them practical experiences in preparation for learning

Slow learners sometimes lack the experience of their brighter classmates, and have no 'concrete empirical props' to support their attempts to grasp concepts.

Use a variety of stimuli
Visits, interesting visitors, vivid visual aids, models, audio and video recordings are valuable stimuli. Emphasis should be onthe simple and appealing, and on the pupils' ability to discriminate, that is, to recognize similarities and differences.

Encourage working as one of a pair
Aim to pair a poor reader with a pupil who can just cope. The poor reader is not overwhelmed and feels able to contribute while the other pupil gains through a sense of responsibility.Learning cooperatively can be very powerful.

Make special arrangements for teacher–pupil contact
The normal arrangement of periodic briefing as a member of a group with occasional *ad hoc* help may have to be overridden. The slow learner's need is for *very frequent*, *short* contacts, in order to get reassurance and specific step-by-step guidance. The feeling of being in personal contact with the teacher is essential.

Use more repetition
Get the pupil to repeat instructions. Allow him to practise a task well beyond the point of initial mastery. Give more examples to illustrate a point.

Improve the pupil's self-image and sense of responsibility
Use praise. Give the pupil a real responsibility in the classroom, for example, something which goes beyond a mere repetitive chore, but which demands some decision-making.

Give special attention to record keeping
Detailed knowledge and awareness can sometimes make the difference between failure and success with these pupils.

Remember that improvements can only be achieved by considering the whole child
Don't be too clinical. Always balance effort directed at cognitive matters with interest and enthusiasm for the physical and social achievements.

Very able pupils

Just like the term 'slow learners' 'very able pupils' is not precise. In no way does it represent a recognizable well-defined group of pupils for which there can be a clearly defined set of needs with an equally clear set of prescriptions. The problem is made more difficult in that many teachers do not recognize very able pupils as easily as they recognize the slow learners. So the first task must be to create greater awareness of pupils who, in one way or another, exhibit talents of an exceptional kind. Table 8.2 provides a checklist of characteristics which may be observed in exceptionally able children.

Table 8.2 *Checklist for use in the study of very able pupils*

1. A marked intellectual curiosity.
2. A capacity to observe intently and in a purposeful way.
3. A capacity for concentration to an unusual degree.
4. The ability to persevere in order to achieve intellectual satisfaction.
5. The ability to use languages, written and spoken, in a sophisticated way.
6. The ability to memorize details.
7. Powers of reasoning beyond their years, particularly in the handling of abstractions.
8. A preference for seeking underlying causes, fundamental principles, and for pursuing back to origins or forward to ultimate outcomes.
9. Well-developed imagination.
10. A wide span of interests.
11. A capacity for organizing their own learning on independent lines.
12. A particular ability in using books as sources of information and inspiration.

Reference must also be made to those pupils who are gifted in a highly specific way, for example, in music, dancing, art, mathematic, team games. These may or may not show some of the other characteristics listed above.

Awareness is the first duty of the teacher, and a constant look-out is necessary. These pupils do not always display their talents in class; they may have learnt to suppress them. Sometimes the clues may come from outside the school, and the teacher needs to be ready to follow them up.

Under-achieving in exceptionally able pupils

The need for identification is more strongly felt when it is recognized that many exceptionally able pupils do in fact *under-achieve* to a considerable degree. The reason can often be traced back to a lack of personal and social adjustment. The bright pupil feels himself to be 'different' and his experiences at the hands of his fellow pupils may confirm that feeling. The indicators of under-achievement are the apparent inconsistencies in the pupil's responses:

● apparently bored and hostile, yet enthusiastic and markedly successful on chosen tasks;

- apparently absorbed in a private world yet suddenly enthusiastic and cooperative on chosen tasks;
- apparently arrogant and tactless, yet able to express a deep sense of personal responsibility;
- apparently unstable, yet able at times to work exceedingly hard in a stimulating way.

Help from outside the classroom

Identification of exceptionally able pupils calls for a whole school approach. There needs to be systematic discussion, agreement about definitions, and a thorough system of records so that progress can be monitored. The teacher who recognizes a very able pupil should be able to call on outside help. Unfortunately, few schools provide specialists in the same way as remedial specialists, but there are ways in which the services of the school can be mobilized.

The school library can be a great source of strength. When a team of teachers has communicated the objectives and content of its courses to the librarian it should be possible for books and other resources to be acquired that help the able pupil go beyond the basic requirements of the course. Such materials would be more advanced in every way—in language, in concepts, and in style. Other 'in-school' arrangements that can help the work of an individual pupil are:

- setting up small groups of able pupils to work on specific tasks together in 'out-of-school' hours;
- withdrawal of able pupils from a number of classes.

Beyond the school itself there are a number of other possible sources of support:

- A number of educational institutions welcome the opportunity to help meet the needs of the brighter pupils of the previous stage. Secondary schools help their local primary schools; and VI Form Colleges, Colleges of Higher Education, and Universities help pupils from secondary schools in their area.
- Specialist organizations often run classes or events for young people, and these are often aimed at the more able. Examples are museums, theatres, community organizations, religious organizational official bodies, industry and commerce.
- Industrial and commercial firms, and public bodies will often give sympathetic reception to a request from an able youngster who wishes to carry out a well-formulated piece of research.

Help from the pupil's regular teacher: suggested techniques
Like the slow learner, the exceptionally able pupil is likely to get most of his help from his regular teacher. A number of practical suggestions follow.

Take great care that any special arrangements which are made help to build up the self-concept of the pupil The able pupil can be sharply critical both of himself and his teacher. He may not necessarily welcome every attempt to provide him with a challenging experience. Great care is needed.

Look outwards for opportunities for the able pupils National or local competitions can provide an incentive (and an excuse!) to get deeply involved in something in their own time. Residential holiday courses provide similar opportunities.

Always collect stimulating resource material which is relevant to the course, even if it seems too difficult for all the pupils A collection of such material is always useful for the teacher's own use. It serves an additional role when it can become a topic for discussion with one or two able pupils.

When a course seems to be well-established, examine the task cards with a view to enriching some of them for the able pupils This may simply mean producing short extension cards which pose problems and provide guides to library materials which might help.

Use an able pupil as a teacher Set a specific task or problem and get the pupil to teach the material found to a small-group.

Get the able pupil to write some additional task cards This, as the teacher will know, is an intellectually demanding exercise. A little coaching, to explain the educational objectives, and some of the contraints, will be most useful, both in terms of the end product, and in terms of the process which the pupil is experiencing.

Take every opportunity to engage the pupil in a discussion about the work To do it properly this needs time and privacy and few teachers would begrudge time in out-of-school hours for this purpose. The able pupil will respond to a more sophisticated use of vocabulary, a genuine sharing of knowledge and experience, a thoughtful and responsible atmosphere, and a sense of equality based on mutual respect.

The teacher's role in individual learning

In a class which is organized for individual learning the main job of the teacher is to *teach*. There is a big temptation to become a busy organizer, attending to a rapid succession of trivial needs. At the end of the lesson the teacher is exhausted, but has made little contact with the pupils in terms of their learning. The teacher may try to rationalize by claiming that the pupils are acquiring the skills of independent study, but, in fact, too much dependence is being placed on the resources and printed guidance. The pupils need the teacher more than they need the resources, therefore, the teacher must create as much time as possible for teaching, and some suggestions about how this might be accomplished were made in Chapter 7.

Teaching activities include the briefing of groups prior to a phase of individual study, the tutoring of individuals or small-groups during individual study, and the responding to requests for help from individual pupils. In Chapter 7 the importance of briefing was emphasized, and the dangers of relying too much on responding to need. Within both of these activities there is tutoring, i.e. the one-to-one contact between teacher and pupil.

Tutoring

This is a sophisticated art, requiring practice, and therefore, worth some detailed analysis. The amount of time that a teacher can create for tutoring is likely to be strictly limited, therefore it must be done well. It is wrong to assume that *any* tutoring, however done, is bound to be good. Unless it is done really well it is better not attempted at all.

Tutoring needs to be intensely personal, and therefore must be conducted with great sensitivity. It is a sort of 'learning conversation' in which the pupil is being helped to be aware of his own stage of development, and to identify for himself how he might develop his understanding. The teacher's job is to listen, to help the pupil to formulate his own statements, to offer reflections and personal support. The aim is to get the 'learning conversation' going on almost entirely inside the pupil's own head, so that he becomes an autonomous learner.

The techniques are sophisticated, and need practice, and it is a pity that the average teacher gets so little opportunity for this because of large classes and a full timetable. Nevertheless, for those who aspire to develop ideas about tutoring, some practical suggestions are provided.

Suggested techniques

Always start by listening   The temptation to 'introduce' or 'get things going' is great but must be resisted. Ask your leading question and then be prepared to *wait*. Do not add supplementary questions too hurriedly, but give a sympathetic gesture, such as a smile or nod of the head, which will often bring out more.

Concentrate, in the early stages, on helping the pupil to articulate his own perceptions more fully   Even if you feel his ideas are wrong or inadequate, it is still important for him to express them in as complete a form as possible. When he has done this you will have a much clearer understanding of where he is now.

Start making your own contributions from 'inside'   Join him, as much as you can, in sympathy, and offer generously your own knowledge, experience, and support.

Encourage him to retain control over his own learning development   The final goal is not to get the pupil to the teacher's level of understanding or point of view, but rather to develop confidence, a sense of personal responsibility, and a feeling of being a self-propelling learner.

Summary

1. Research suggests that individuals think and learn in different ways.
2. Response by the teacher should be a judicious blend of respect for an individual's personal style with discreet strategies for enlarging the repertoire.
3. Exceptional pupils in the regular class highlight the problems of individual learning. There is a trend towards mainstreaming, with various degrees of withdrawal.
    Slow learners need adaptations which emphasize:
   - relationships;
   - home contacts;
   - variety of stimuli;
   - practical 'pre-academic' experiences;
   - working in a partnership;
   - more frequent, short teacher contacts;
   - more repetition;
   - 'self-image' and a sense of responsibility;
   - record keeping;
   - the whole child.

Exceptionally able pupils need adaptations which emphasize:

- the pupil's self-concept;
- stimulus from outside the school;
- advanced resource material;
- enriched guidance materials;
- the pupil as a teacher;
- the pupil involved in the intellectual tasks associated with course planning and preparation;
- extended conversations (out of hours) with the teacher.

4. The Teacher's role in individual learning. The art of tutoring is sophisticated and requires practice.

It is intensely personal and consists of a 'learning conversation' in which the pupil is being helped to be aware of his own development.

9. The techniques of small-group work

The purpose of this chapter is to consider the role of the small-group in the classroom setting. The discussion will be confined to the small-group of four, five, or six pupils, since discussions of the larger groupings of the whole class and division and of the small grouping of the pair have already taken place.In order to make the most effective use of the small-group in teaching and learning we need to answer four questions. First, we need to know the *purposes and functions* appropriate for the small-group techniques. Second, we need to examine more closely the decisions that the teacher has to make about the *structures* of small groups. Third, we need to consider what are the most suitable *occasions* for small-group work. Finally, we need to look at the *processes and techniques* which are appropriate in the small-group situation.

The purposes and functions of small-groups

The underlying purpose of small-group work is to increase the opportunities for pupil–pupil interaction. When pupils are talking to each other about their work, in the absence of the teacher, the situation is full of potential for learning. Each individual pupil begins at his own starting point. He may already have some relevant knowledge which he can bring to bear or he may be starting in complete ignorance. He may have some attitudes to the work in hand which are bound to affect his thinking and his contributions. He may have attitudes towards himself which will affect his self-confidence and his motivation.

Whatever his starting point, the individual pupil will influence the direction which the group work takes. As a participating member of the group he will help to set the pace, to ask the questions, to formulate the answers, and to criticize the general direction of the argument. It is through this process that the pupil is helped to assume a responsibility for his own learning, and to develop a real sense of *ownership* of new knowledge and understanding. The knowledge has become *personal* knowledge, through the participation, involvement, and commitment of the learner.

This is the justification for increasing the amount of pupil–pupil interaction through small-group work, although the picture presented is idealized. Teachers will recognize that it is bound to be a slow way of learning, and that it may not reach the conclusions and vocabulary that the teacher wants.The temptation is always to intervene, and to 'get them on the right track'. But this would be an unfortunate judgement. The pupils need time to express themselves in their own way, to explore ideas, to use their imagination, to share in the formulation of ideas and solutions to problems, and to plan and organize the work of the group. This is not to imply that the teacher should totally abdicate during periods of small-group activity. Preparation, follow up and timely intervention are all vital. Sensitivity is the keyword for the teacher.

Small-group work, emphasizing pupil–pupil interaction, can be used as a vehicle in the pursuit of many different kinds of educational objectives. But it is at its best when the activity centres on one of the following:

- communicating;
- cooperating;
- competing.

Communicating

This overlaps with the other two headings. Examples of communication activities within the small-group learning situation are described below.

1. Individual members of the group make reports to the group (e.g., on some private research or reading, or on some practical observations or experience).
2. Individual members present questions or problems for the whole group to consider.
3. Individual members present test questions on newly learnt material for group members to answer.
4. The group tries to identify an 'animal, vegetable, or mineral' selected by one member from the topic being studied. Since questions can only be answered by 'yes' or 'no', there is much skill in formulating questions, and advancing in a systematic way.
5. The group holds a discussion to make decisions based on evidence supplied.
6. The group holds a discussion to propose solutions to a set problem.
7. The group holds a discussion to make a judgement on an issue presented to them (short case-studies lend themselves to this approach particularly well).
8. The group holds a 'brainstorm'. This is a way of quickly producing a *large* number of ideas or approaches to a problem, in which novelty and variety (even eccentricity) are encouraged but criticism (at this stage) is not allowed. This is an excellent 'starter' technique.

Cooperating

This is bound to involve a lot of communicating, but the emphasis is on the joint production of something worth while.

1. The group works collaboratively to make a presentation for exhibition or display.
2. The group works collaboratively to make a dramatic presentation, for example, an audio-tape, an informal role play.
3. The group works collaboratively to produce a joint report for oral presentation.
4. The group acts as a consultant. Each member brings a difficulty or problem which he has experienced in the topic being studied. The group offers help and guidance.
5. The group prepares for a 'negotiation' with another group. This could be a simple debate or a simulation activity.
6. The group studies a prepared simulation which involves studying the prepared data together, and discussing responses.

Competing

Again, a lot of communicating is involved.

1. Individuals compete against each other in a prepared game.
2. Two sides are formed to run a question and answer competition.
3. Charades and similar role-playing games can be organized on a competitive basis.

The structure of small-groups

This is represented by a set of important decisions that the teacher has to make at the outset. The decisions made can affect the organization and smooth running of the lessons. They can also affect the educational outcomes of the lessons in both the cognitive sense and also in the attitudes and interpersonal relations which are formed.

Group size

We have already argued the case for an optimum size of five for a small-group, on the grounds that this seems to be a minimum to ensure a reasonable variety of input into a discussion, and a maximum to ensure that all members take an active part. There is an advantage too in the odd number, so that whenever a disagreement is being examined the group is spared the dilemma of being locked in two intransigent sides.

Some careful research has been done on the question of group size, and it has confirmed that as the size increased the differences between the contributions of the dominant member and the most withdrawn member increases rapidly.In one piece of research the most talkative member contributed about 40 per cent of the total communication *whatever the size of the group.*

Another good argument for keeping the group size down to five is that as the group gets bigger, problems of procedure begin to interfere with the work. Much time has to be spent deciding how the group is going to decide! Adults will often play these committee games quite happily for hours on end, but young people tend to get restless and discipline problems follow.Two factors may legitimately persuade us against a too rigid adherence to the magic figure of five. First, the odd number creates a complication in a class which is making heavy use of the pair as a working unit. When pairs combine to form a small-group one pair must be broken up. For this reason some teachers, who have a strong commitment to small-group work, might be better advised to abandon pairs altogether, relying on a blend of individual work and small-group work. The alternative is to form small-groups of four or six pupils. Second, there may be a number of occasions when the small-group of five members is not likely to contain the necessary skills for the task that has been set. Sometimes large groups can be a powerful way of tackling quite difficult problems, provided there are enough pacesetters within the group. Admittedly in this situation some group members will not be so active, but will get the benefit of being in the discussion. It is a good model, but only *occasionally.*

Group composition

There are two questions to be decided on group composition. Should the groups be homogeneous or heterogeneous? Who should determine the membership of the groups, the teacher or the pupil? The evidence is that homogeneous groups tend to get away to an easy start. The similarities among the members ensure that interpersonal conflicts are likely to be kept to a minimum. On the other hand, a heterogeneous group seems to bring a wide range of perspective on a topic and may often produce wise decisions, particularly in the areas of problem-solving and value judgements. Moreover, the very process of interaction between pupils of differing backgrounds and abilities is in itself part of the process of education. If interpersonal relationships are improved in the small-group setting, then the method is a powerful one indeed.

In practical terms, this might best be implemented by allowing the pair to be reasonably homogeneous, but to accept a certain amount of heterogeneity in the composition of the small-group. It is an advantage if the small-group can be mixed sex. Who should decide the membership? Probably the teacher will wish to retain the right to veto, but experience suggests that pupils pair themselves well on the basis of friendship, and this usually works out satisfactorily because of roughly comparable skills and shared attitudes and standards. The formation of the small-groups will probably require only the minimum intervention by the teacher, where, for example, two pairs of rather slow pupils wish to form a group.

Leadership

Should the teacher assume a leadership role in the small-group work? Or should pupils be appointed to perform the duties? Or should the small-groups be allowed to operate as leaderless groups? The teacher's involvement clearly depends on his being able to arrange the working of the whole class so that he can be spared to devote a reasonable amount of time to one small-group. This is not likely to be achieved very often, but when it happens it is very important for the teacher to adopt the role of a supporting chairman in preference to that of a task leader. This means encouraging individuals to contribute, fostering a sense of group cohesion, and maintaining a positive atmosphere directed at the task goals. It also means playing down one's own information, ideas, experience, and opinions.

For most occasions, however, it must be assumed that it is both necessary and desirable that the leadership should be in the hands of the pupils themselves. An appointed leader can considerably enhance the achievements of a group, but equally it can be a disaster for the group. An appointed leader makes or breaks the group. So the use of appointed leaders requires careful *selection and training*. Quite young pupils can be trained in some of the essentials of group leadership provided sufficient time can be found. They need to be taught how to apply simple rules of procedure, how to move the discussion along by asking stimulating and exploratory questions, how to keep reminding the group of its goals. The emphasis, as in the case of the teacher, should be on the supporting chairman role rather than on the task leader role.

There is a strong case for the small-group of four, five, or six pupils to be constituted without a formally designated leader. Leadership is likely to emerge quite naturally. It will not be concentrated in the hands of one member. It will come from different members at different times and for different purposes. One member may lead in information-giving;

another in imaginative thinking; another by forcefully making assertions which give the group something to 'bite on', another may be the conciliator, that is, the one who is more concerned with keeping the group in harmony so that the work will be completed.

A further important advantage of the 'leaderless' group is that in the event of a breakdown the teacher can intervene without the intervention being seen as a personal criticism of an appointed leader.

Occasions and situations for small-groups

This section attempts to answer the questions: where? and when? We should not assume that small-group work always takes place within the four walls of the self-contained classroom. During the 1960s, with the developments in team teaching, many new schools were designed as open-plan schools. The emphasis was on cooperative planning by a team of teachers and flexibility in the grouping arrangements. Although there has been a reaction against the open-plan architecture, the educational principles of team teaching retain a strong influence. There is today much simple cooperation between teachers and their classes, and the members of the class frequently spill out of the classroom into spare seminar rooms or into corners in the corridors or cloakrooms. There is much to be said for this so that the members of the group can talk freely without feeling that they are disrupting the individual work which may be going on in the classroom. Success depends on clear briefing of the group about the tasks, procedures, and outcomes, and a clear understanding about standards of behaviour and the rules of debate.

Many small-groups will, of necessity, be confined to the classroom. They should be encouraged to sit as closely to each other as possible, in a circle or round a single table, the principle being that eye contact increases communication among group members. So, ideally, the least talkative should directly face the most talkative; and the two most talkative pupils should sit alongside each other. The teacher is likely to be far too busy to spend time working out optimum seating arrangement, but sometimes a single intervention can make a difference to the pattern of communication.

Generally it is better if each small-group operates within its own home base. This means that a group can re-form itself and get down to business with the minimum disturbance of the rest of the class. Some teachers, however, prefer to have a part of the classroom screened off for group discussions.

When are the best times for small-group work? This has already been answered in one way by our consideration of the purposes and functions of small-group work. But purely in terms of time, the group work should logically come at a late stage in the course of studies. In the early stages pupils have a need for general orientation and stimulus and motivation, and this can be best provided by the teacher. Then there is a stage at which more information is accumulated, ideas developed, observations and experiences enlarged, and this can often be done best by individual working. Group work comes most appropriately when the individual members of the group are *ready*. This state of readiness is reached when one or more of the following has happened:

- Pupils have spent some time working on their own, finding out information, developing ideas or practising skills.
- Pupils have received a common stimulus during which there has been no opportunity for them to react, other than privately, e.g., viewing a film, listening to a live radio broadcast, a theatre visit.
- Pupils have shared a common experience where there has been much opportunity for individual observation and personal reflection, e.g., an educational visit.
- Pupils are known to have had some personal experiences in their out-of-school lives which will have some bearing on the work theme.

The principle is that there can be no worthwhile group work until the individual members can bring to the group their individual and *different* knowledge, observations, experiences, perceptions, and attitudes.

The processes and techniques of small-group work

Successful small-group work requires careful preparation by the teacher followed by a continuous effort to improve the discussion skills of the participants.

Preparation

It must be the teacher's first duty to build up the confidence of the pupils in their own competence as members of a group. This depends very much on how the teacher operates within the class as a whole. If the teacher–pupil relationship is dominated by the teacher's own perceptions about goals, and about procedures, it is unlikely that pupils will develop a sufficiently serious regard for their own contributions when it comes to group work. To get the sense of responsibility and confidence which is required, the teacher must demonstrate at all times that the pupil's views are listened to and respected. This does not necessarily mean that they are accepted, but it does mean that the teacher perceives every pupil's contribution to a discussion as an opportunity for learning.

119

To build a pupil's self-respect in this way may mean a deferment of criticism about vocabulary, style, dialect, and accent. The need at this stage is to get the pupil started on the journey, not to attempt to get there all in one move.

In discussion about the learning programme the teacher should clearly explain the role of the small-group and stress its importance. If the teacher believes in the method and has high expectations of it, it is likely that pupils will have similar feelings.

Immediately prior to a small-group activity there would be a briefing session as described in Chapter 7. This should be an opportunity to reaffirm the value placed on the work of the group, but the main task would be to establish objectives and give guidance about procedures. While it would be wrong to specify exactly what the results of the work should be, there should nevertheless be a clear statement about what form the results should take and about their presentation. It is worth taking time over this, and getting pupils to ask questions and offer suggestions, before finally summing up.

In a similar way the guidance about procedures must be detailed and thorough. The teacher must strike a balance between the prescriptive and the *laissez-faire*; it is not easy and the balance must reflect the unique situation of the group. It is best to give a model procedure, suggesting the stages through which the group might work, some of the questions to be asked, the way that conclusions or decisions might be presented. But throughout, emphasis should be placed on the personal contributions of the individual members.

Finally the 'house rules' must be firmly stated. These cover location, time-scale, noise-level, and general discipline.

An additional preparatory activity is for the teacher to ensure that the group will have access to any necessary resources. This has probably been catered for in the general preparation of course materials, but it is particularly important in group work involving difficult decisions or problems.

Interventions

When the small-group has assembled for its tasks things get really difficult for the teacher. On the one hand, the teacher needs to stay away so that the pupils develop their own strategies and come to their own conclusions. On the other hand, the teacher has a responsibility to give guidance and help, to set standards, and to ensure that the group keeps on course. It is worth eavesdropping occasionally, but intervening only rarely. Being asked for specific help for clarification is another matter and should be welcomed.

Table 9.1 *Small-group questionnaire*

Read each statement carefully.
Do *you* think it is TRUE or FALSE?
Mark your choice with a tick.

1. I had a clear understanding at the beginning of *what* the group had to do.	TRUE	FALSE
2. I had a clear understanding at the beginning about *how* we were to set about it.	TRUE	FALSE
3. All the members of the group took part in the discussion.	TRUE	FALSE
4. One member of the group did too much of the talking.	TRUE	FALSE
5. Most of the good ideas came from one member.	TRUE	FALSE
6. The group members were cooperative towards each other rather than competitive.	TRUE	FALSE
7. Some members of the group formed themselves into a clique.	TRUE	FALSE
8. Some members of the group prevented us from making progress.	TRUE	FALSE
9. We found the rules for the discussion very useful.	TRUE	FALSE
10. This was an enjoyable experience.	TRUE	FALSE
11. We could have got better results by working individually.	TRUE	FALSE
12. The experience made me think.	TRUE	FALSE

Now complete each of these statements in your own way.

1. I think the best things about this group work were:

....

....

....

2. Next time we do group work I should like to see the following improvements:

....

....

....

Reporting

This is a useful element in any brief for a small-group. It demands that the private, informal, exploratory talk should lead eventually to presentation which will be public, formal, and conclusive. This is a challenge to the group and it will contribute to group cohesion and give a sense of purpose. Pupils should be encouraged to put themselves in the place of their audience when they are preparing their presentation.

Analysis and evaluation

The teacher needs to extend still further his own opportunities for influencing the styles of the small-group and for developing the skills of individual participants. A useful way of doing this is to build in some analysis and evaluation for each small-group session. A simple questionnaire which individuals complete at the end of the session could form the basis for subsequent class discussions on small-group work. This will emphasize again the importance attached to the group work, and focus attention of the group processes and the skills which the pupils are developing. An example of such a questionnaire, suitable for 10-12 year old pupils, is shown in Table 9.1.

After the teacher has had time to study responses from a number of groups the stage is set for a class discussion. This can focus not only on the specific tasks which the groups have just undertaken, but also on the small-group method in general. Taken seriously, this can help raise the standards of group work by alerting the teacher to weaknesses in the task content and procedures, and by emphasizing again to the pupils the importance of the method and how they might improve their own personal performances as members of the group. So much of adult life is spent in making group decisions, in working as a member of a team, in responding to group pressures, that it is worth re-emphasizing that the skills involved in group work constitute a set of educational objectives in their own right.

Summary

The small-group is an important unit in the organization of pupils' learning.

Purposes and functions   There are three main purposes:
1. Communicating: reporting, questioning, discussing, problem-solving, evaluating, speculating, exploring.

2. Cooperating: the preparing of visual presentations, dramatic presentations, joint reports, negotiating positions, consulting, preparing responses to simulations.
3. Competing: games, quizzes, role-playing.

Structure   There are three important considerations:
1. Size: the case has been made for a normal optimum of five members, but variations from this can occasionally be justified.
2. Composition: there are advantages in homogeneous groups and in heterogeneous groups. On balance there is probably more *potential* in the heterogeneous group. Pupil choice of partnership arrangements often work out quite well with minimum teacher intervention. But the teacher should guard against members of a pair being too dissimilar in performance and attitude.
3. Leadership: normally leaderless small-groups work well. Leaders of different kinds may emerge when the need is apparent, and the teacher can always intervene in a helpful way if the situation seems to require it.

Occasions and situations   Small-group work *outside* the four walls of the classroom has much to commend it. Physical arrangement of the small-group in session should be planned for maximum participation of all members. Generally the small-group work comes *late* in a cycle of learning, when the pupils have acquired the necessary information, ideas, observations and experiences.

Processes and techniques   Preparation for group work is an important task for the teacher. The class needs to be *ready* psychologically for the experience. Intervention by the teacher needs to be sensitively undertaken.

10. The pupils' behaviour

The purpose of this chapter is to look at the problem of the pupils' behaviour in the classroom and to examine ways in which the teacher might more effectively cope.

There has been much publicity in recent years which claims that standards of discipline in the schools have declined. The focus has been on aggressive and disruptive behaviour; acts of violence against persons and property; drug abuse; use of alcohol; truancy, defiance of authority; stealing. Many teachers have to spend a disproportionate amount of their time dealing with delinquent pupils and the consequences of their actions.

Teachers generally agree that standards are more difficult to maintain now, and would add to the list many other manifestations which do not make headlines, but which do make the teacher's work much more difficult: boredom; unwillingness to cooperate; anxiety; indifferent health; and a host of other symptoms of underlying distress. Whatever legislation may be passed, whatever improvements may be made in welfare services, whatever efforts are made by the media to alert the community as a whole, the fact remains that it is the teacher in the classroom who becomes most acutely aware of the total problem, and who bears the almost impossible burden of trying to cope with so many different needs.

There are some who, in the face of all these problems, have abandoned educational objectives in favour of counselling and crisis management. They argue that it is impossible to teach these pupils anything until their personal lives have been sorted out. The trouble is that this is never achieved. There are others who declare themselves to be teachers, not social workers, hoping that the problems will go away, or that somebody else will deal with them. There is a third group, and they are probably the majority, who are desperately torn between the two points of view outlined above. They appreciate that children's lives cannot be compartmentalized, and that success can only occur across a wide front embracing every aspect of a pupil's life and development. And the solutions are not easy.

The causes of the problems

It is not within the scope of this book to attempt a thorough analysis of the likely causes of disruptive and uncooperative behaviour in schools, but a short summary of some of the arguments about underlying causes will help to illuminate the problems in preparation for a discussion of classroom strategies.

Most of the causes of disruptive and uncooperative behaviour can be traced back to four main sources: society as a whole, the home, the school, and adolescence.

Society as a whole

We are not entirely on firm ground when we try to ascribe failures in behaviour to general conditions which pertain in society as a whole. The assertions, outlined below, are often difficult to prove, though many appear to be based on observation, common sense, and logic.

- The present economic problems of the country have seriously reduced the individual's feeling of personal financial security.
- Most of our organizations are bigger, and seem to offer less scope for individuality.
- Nuclear warfare remains as an underlying threat to all mankind.
- The advance of technology is perceived by many as a threat to jobs and to personal dignity.
- There has been an increased use of violence by small groups in order to attain political or personal gain.
- The decay of inner city areas has proceeded faster than the measures to combat it.
- Unfair discrimination is still a feature of our society.

It is possible to make direct connections between some of these factors and the disaffected youth in our schools. Many black youths *perceive* a discrimination against them by the white community, many young people in inner city areas *perceive* a discrimination against them on the part of the police. Other connections are less easy to make, but it seems to be a reasonable general proposition that modern youth is growing up in a world beset by problems which society seems unable to resolve. This may seem to be a dispiriting starting point for the individual teacher, but these are the social realities with which the teaching profession will have to contend. The whole of our planning and teaching must be guided by a realization of the sheer size of the 'coping' task which has to be performed by our young people.

The home

The home can be to blame for neglect, which may be physical, or mental, or emotional, or a combination of these. Physical neglect may include neglect of meals, clothing, and health. Mental neglect may include an absence of conversation (language deprivation), a contempt for anything remotely intellectual, the determined exclusion of rationality as a basis of decision-making. Emotional neglect may include depravity in the home, emotional violence and cruelty, mental abnormality in the home, a lack of love and of a sense of security. The underlying causes of these aspects of neglect are invariably to be found with the parents. The cycle of neglect is a continuous one which schools have found difficult to break. Fortunately, there are enough people who believe that schools can make a difference.

The school

The school itself may be a source of problems for a school can easily give an impression of being impersonal and insensitive. It may give an impression that it cares little for those who are not distinguished intellectually. It may display a distrust of its pupils through a number of minor rules and regulations and in its conventions, it may regularly stifle initiative and self-confidence. It may show little respect for the opinions or feelings of its pupils. In countless ways neglect may show, and it may all be done with the best intentions.

It is not wise to be complacent in this matter. A school needs to review regularly all its policies, rules, procedures, and conventions, asking the simple question: does this arrangement implicitly tell the pupils that they are not respected, trusted, or even liked? Whenever the answer is in the affirmative the difficult task of devising alternative arrangements begins. The aim must be to demonstrate respect and trust and to use *that* as the foundation on which good discipline will be built.

Adolescence

Adolescents account for a high proportion of the petty crime which is committed, and it is generally agreed that they constitute a much more serious discipline problem in schools than the younger age groups. It seems reasonable, therefore, to look at the nature of adolescence.

Psychologists emphasize that this is a transitional period during which the young person must start adjusting to the physical changes of adolescence. This implies a new understanding of oneself, the building of new styles of behaviour, the establishment of new relationships with individual people and with society generally, the acquiring of new intellectual capabilities. This is a complex set of tasks, and a certain amount of strain can be expected. We should not be surprised that this strain frequently manifests itself in deviant behaviour.

The infuriating characteristic of many adolescents is their inconsistency. They do not progress smoothly in their efforts to become adults; periods of solid progress are often punctuated by regression, when childlike behaviour or total irresponsibility takes over. This should be interpreted as a trial and error approach to self-discovery. The drive towards independence is very strong, and the young pupil simply has to experiment with his own developing powers in order to acquire a basis of experience on which to base future action. It can be very disconcerting for the parent and the teacher. The two need to work together very closely, avoiding at all costs the mutual recriminations which so often attend home–school crises. The adolescent needs help in establishing his own identity, and the help must come from parents, teachers, and the community at large.

One of the more difficult aspects of the problem of adolescence is the existence of the youth subculture as distinct from the adult culture. The adolescent is acutely aware of this and wants to preserve 'the generation gap', relying more heavily on the judgements and values of the peer group. Teachers in secondary schools have to learn that 11-year-olds who relate so well to them when they first arrive in the school will change within a few years. They become withdrawn and are unwilling to be seen in too close harmony with their teachers. The wise teacher uses peer-group approval as part of his armoury, and does not seek approval and adoration for himself!

Classroom strategies

Success in building up a good standard of discipline depends on both long-term strategies, and immediate or short-term tactics. The long-term strategies are based on a good knowledge of the educational and social contact within which the teaching takes place. We have already examined the possible sources of behaviour problems, i.e., the state of our present society, the home, the school, and the nature of adolescence. The teacher must be knowledgeable in these areas both in a general sense and specifically with regard to his own pupils. Much writing about education in recent years has had a sociological orientation, and much discussion by the media has reflected this. So there is no shortage of data and of interpretation and opinion. Today's teacher has a better chance than his predecessors of being 'in touch' with the world of his pupils, at least in a vicarious way. This wealth of information has its dangers: that of teachers who know *about* the problems and are eloquent in discussion, but who are reluctant to work out *how* to respond to them and even more reluctant to face up to the practical difficulties involved.

Acquiring specific knowledge

The first step is to make the knowledge much more specific. This means developing a sensitive understanding of the catchment area of the school, building up good home–school relationships, and building up good knowledge about individual pupils. This depends to some extent on a good system of school records to which the teacher has access, but there is more to it than this. The main virtues of many long-standing members of the profession is their encyclopaedic knowledge of the people, the places, the institutions, and the history of the local area. They know the pupils' families. Knowledge of this kind is the first weapon in the teacher's armoury.

Thorough preparation

The second weapon is thorough preparation. We have already devoted a whole chapter to the preparation of course materials and another to the preparation of the classroom. These must be re-emphasized for the support they give to the building of good discipline standards. The teacher who is plainly 'filling in time', or having to change activities because materials cannot be found, or is not prepared for problems which pupils encounter, is on a slippery downward slope. A pupil gets a sense of stability and purpose from a realization that the teacher's preparation is well ahead of his needs. Respect for the teacher follows automatically.

The teacher also needs to be well prepared in those matters which are directly concerned with standards of discipline. If there is a code of school rules, the teacher should know them well enough to be able to apply them without hesitation. The same applies to administrative procedures which have been laid down in the school to ensure orderly movement, care of premises, and so on. The same applies also to schemes of rewards and punishments. The teacher must know them all well so that they can be applied easily and naturally without hesitation. A teacher should not allow his own personal attitude to school rules and procedures to get in the way. To subvert in any way, through explicit verbal disagreement or through implicit action or lack of it, is to undermine his own discipline and the discipline of the whole school. If the teacher disagrees with the rules or arrangements, he must work to get them changed. This might be a hard cross to bear, where the teacher's personal convictions are strong, and the school somehow intransigent. But there really is no other solution—except to leave, of course!

Image-building

The third strategic weapon is the teacher's image. Pupils tune in to the image which the teacher presents to them from his very first appearance. Subconsciously they watch and record every initiative, every reaction, every expression of feeling. They process all the impressions and form an image which guides all their future behaviour in the teacher's presence. So it is worth while for the teacher to give some thought to image-building.

The first important component is the knowledge which has already been discussed. Pupils must feel that the teacher *knows* about themselves, their families, their home area, that the teacher knows about the school and how to use its systems and procedures, that the teacher *knows* what he is going to teach and has made thorough preparation for it. This has to be achieved step by step over the years, and the beginner may feel at a disadvantage. It is a useful strategy for a beginner to drive a few spearheads into the knowledge problem in order to show the pupils what kind of a teacher they are dealing with. Find an opportunity to demonstrate knowledge of a significant achievement of his family. Find an opportunity to demonstrate knowledge of significant events in the local area or in the school itself. A little name-dropping (small doses only) can often help establish the idea that you know the people and the system: 'The Head said to me yesterday that . . .'.

The second important component in image-building is a serious and firm impression of purpose. It is this intention which is behind the old, apparently cynical, advice: 'Don't smile until Christmas.' It should not be taken literally, but it is a warning to the newcomer (experienced or otherwise) not to seek quick and easy popularity through ingratiating practices or by trying to be 'with-it'. It can fade so quickly. Pupils come to like their teachers by first respecting them, and then happily discovering that they are also very human. The serious and firm impression of purpose is conveyed by being thorough both in one's own contributions and in the demands made on the pupils. This means attention to detail, and an assumption that pupils will take their work seriously and with a sense of responsibility.

The third component is an impression of strength and resolution. The teacher's normal aspect should be calm, pleasant and courteous. Pupils do need to know, however, how the teacher will react in crisis. The newcomer should be ready to demonstrate, on the *first* occasion that it becomes necessary, that he will not flinch from his responsibilities, and that he will be somewhat contemptuous of any attempt to start 'negotiations' after there has been a clear breach of rules or instructions.

The fourth component is an impression of a caring adult. Every opportunity should be taken, and it usually has to be outside the classroom, of establishing some *personal* contact with as many individual pupils as possible. The discovery of a shared interest, a word of praise after an achievement, a word of sympathy after a disappointment, a little practical help or advice, an appreciative word to a parent (who is sure to pass it on), can all help to establish a bond. Most teachers can recall instances of much-improved relationships with pupils after they have shared with them some informal activity such as camping, expeditions, social work, and sporting activities.

Classroom tactics

Strategy and tactics are mutually supportive. Each helps the other; each depends on the other. A sound set of long-term strategies can help a teacher build up good standards of discipline. And the stronger those are the less likely is the need for explicit disciplinary action in the classroom. Nevertheless, teachers are dealing with young people who may not be capable of coping with all the stresses of their lives and who often react by laziness, insubordination, defiance, mischief, aggression, or destructiveness. Tactics in the classroom are designed to avoid or prevent these troubles, or if they do occur, to handle them in the most effective way.

Unfortunately, advice about tactics is less reliable than advice about general strategies. The complexity of classroom life is responsible for this. Classroom life is multidimensional, with many different kinds of activities, many different purposes, and many people having different needs and different styles. Things happen simultaneously. There is an air of immediacy about the place. At any one time the teacher is considering what next to say, thinking ahead about the development of the lesson, watching the progress of pupils, looking out for anything which might disrupt the smooth flow of the work. And then there are the unpredictables, such as the interruption from outside, the unforeseen difficulties, and the minor accidents. In this sort of context the teacher really is thinking on his feet. Much of his action and reaction approaches the intuitive. Deliberate reflective thinking about alternative courses of action is impossible.

Another factor that makes advice about classroom tactics somewhat unreliable is the fact that different teachers can use apparently contradictory tactics with equal success! When a group of teachers is discussing tactics, one teacher's meat is often another teacher's poison.

So suggestions must be offered on a tentative basis, recognizing that many of the suggestions are based on subjective experience, have not been tested by research, and might well be anathema to some teachers. It is simply hoped that suggestions may prove to be useful to *some* teachers.

Design and establish good starting routines for lessons

Good preparation of the room and the materials is part of this and has already been emphasized. It is better if the teacher arrives before the pupils (absolutely essential though for beginners and teachers having difficulty).

The pupils should be *taught* what is expected of them on arrival, i.e., what is to be done without waiting for instructions. For class teaching the instruction might be: 'Collect a copy of each item laid out on the resources table near the door. Have exercise book open and ready.' For individual working the instructions might simply be: 'Collect the materials you are currently working on and resume work.' The teacher's role at the start of the lesson should be purely supervisory and pupils should be instructed to defer any individual approach to the teacher, except in emergency, of course. A clear signal should be agreed which indicates the end of this brief but vital period. During this supervision the teacher controls as much as possible by the eyes, watching all, but focusing especially on those who are dawdling. Avoid speaking if at all possible. The eyes and a few hand gestures will produce most of the desired results.

This can give a quiet, businesslike and disciplined beginning to the lesson. But pupils do need to be *taught* this; and the teacher must resist the temptation to respond to the pupil who breaks the rule and makes an approach. The wait will not be long and learning to work within a framework of rules which do not always satisfy one's own needs immediately is an important lesson.

Establish a clear understanding about 'speaking' rules

First is the need for the teacher to establish beyond any shadow of doubt or question the occasions when he wishes to speak to the class without interruption. Again, pupils need to be *taught* these rules and given practice in them. The signal will usually be a simple verbal request such as 'Everyone pay attention please.' The words should always be the same. It is fatal to attempt to go on by raising one's voice above the level of the pupils' conversation. There will be a natural escalation and this leads to shouting on both sides! The pupils' conversation is not the only problem. A pen or a pencil held in the hand will tempt a pupil to resume writing while the teacher is speaking, or worse, to tap out a little rhythm on the desk top! So the command must mean not only that conversation should cease but also that hands should be empty. All this is so important that it is worth giving up time to establish and periodically reinforce the procedure. Young pupils will enjoy practising it; older pupils met for the first time need to be handled carefully and the procedure presented in terms of 'the rules of debate'.

Second, for class teaching and discussion, there needs to be a clear understanding about the procedure for the pupil to speak. Some experienced teachers can control a class discussion without a 'hands up' procedure; others find it essential. Whatever procedure is adopted it should be clearly explained and then enforced. During discussions, as opposed to teacher's questioning, there is a lot to be said for 'the rules of debate' in order to keep the discussion orderly. Pupils should be taught the forms of words involved in addressing all remarks to the chairman: 'Mr Chairman, I should like Bill to explain . . .'.

Develop clear routines for accomplishing regular organizational tasks

These include taking the roll (if this is required), distributing materials in class teaching, clearing away at the end of lessons, forming groups, using apparatus. The object is to accomplish the task on a single command, everyone knowing clearly his own responsibilities and duties.

Adopt a purely supervisory role at regular intervals throughout a lesson

The teacher is really supervising all the time, and a good teacher is said to have eyes 'in the back of his head'. Nevertheless, it is possible to become thoroughly absorbed in briefing a group, or tutoring, and if this is allowed to go on too long, standards in the room will begin to slip. It is a sort of ripple effect: one or two pupils stop work or raise their voices and the habit quickly spreads. The teacher can prevent this by a short supervisory stint, which can be a quick visual scan of the whole room with a brief, but *unobtrusive*, intervention where there seems to be a slackening of effort. Or it can be a brisk tour of the room to check that all are on task and that no serious deviations have occurred.

All control actions should be as unobtrusive as possible

Effective teachers can wither with a glance! It is worth practising. Equally, gestures and signals can be effective, e.g., a finger to the lips, a hand signal to sit down, a finger to beckon, a nod of approval to allow something to happen, a shake of the head to forbid it, a shake of the head to signal disapproval, an arm akimbo to signal patience getting low. If it is really necessary to speak, approach the pupil and do it *sotto voce*. More can be accomplished this way because the pupil does not lose face and is able to accept the reprimand without a need to retaliate. It is not wise to disturb the whole class, but much better to try to get matters right by tackling the worst offenders privately. If the general noise level has a habit of escalating (and it usually has), check it early on as unobtrusively as possible. 'Shsh' can work wonders! 'A quiet teacher makes a quiet class.'

Continue to demonstrate your 'knowledge'

Always use a pupil's name. Make each exchange as personal as possible. Be friendly and constructive.

Maintain the momentum and smoothness of the lesson

Keep up the pace of the activity and learning. Do not do anything which will slow it down. Being long-winded can take away the momentum of a lesson: 'going-on' about a pupil's misbehaviour; over-elaborating an anecdote; over-teaching the obvious instead of getting on to some thing of more substance.

A lesson can lose its smoothness by the teacher allowing irrelevant business into the lesson, by perpetually interrupting pupils' work with instructions or exhortations to the whole class just because one pupil seemed to need it, or by 'chopping and changing' one activity for another.

Sensitivity to the need for momentum and smoothness can do a great deal to keep pupils on task and well-behaved.

Anticipate discipline problems and act quickly and decisively

Alertness, anticipation, quick recognition, prompt but unobtrusive action are the characteristics of the good disciplinarian. Where the teacher is uncertain it is wise not to hesitate but to intervene in a non-critical way. Ask the pupil to explain what progress he has made or

133

what problem he has encountered. This gets him on to the task without accusing him purely on the basis of hunch.

Where the misbehaviour is overt and of a slightly defiant nature, the decisive action is to remove the pupil from his audience. Take him to another part of the room to speak to him, and let him stay there to do his next task. Once you have made a decision do not regard it as negotiable. For that reason it is important to build into the decision a clear end of the sanction. This helps the pupil to accept it or, putting it another way, gives him less cause for defiant refusal.

Avoid confrontation

Confrontation is public and emotionally charged. It can result in frightful escalation with an unwillingness to back down on either side. It is watched with fascination by the rest of the class (who have stopped work) and their judgement at the end, whatever the outcome, will be against the teacher. An openly defiant pupil should be removed from the classroom and it is to be hoped that most schools would have arrangements so that this could be arranged with supervision. The teacher will then have the opportunity to deal with the problem privately and (probably by then) more calmly.

The disruptive pupil

Many classes contain one or two pupils who are constantly disruptive. They exhibit symptoms of at least a slight degree of maladjustment. They are unable to concentrate or persevere; they are noisy, they are physically restless, inclined to interfere with other pupils and provoke them; they are quarrelsome; they react emotionally and start a tantrum if they are reprimanded; they get bored easily and are easily defeated by difficulties; they usually believe that they are being victimized; they often want to be friendly to the teacher but seem unable to prevent themselves being cheeky or silly. They can do an immense amount of harm in a classroom.

Although other pupils may not respect them, they are nevertheless influenced by them. The teacher has to spend a disproportionate amount of time restraining them, and, all too frequently, confrontations occur which bring an abrupt halt to the work of the whole class. How can the teacher possibly cope?

The main problem for the teacher is how to allocate time and effort. On the one hand, there is an educational programme and a class of pupils who need help and guidance; on the other hand there is the disruptive pupil who needs special attention. It would be totally wrong for the teacher to become so wrapped up with the problems of the disruptive pupil that the needs of the rest were neglected. It is wrong for the teacher to try to assume the role of therapist or social worker. The teacher's duty is to maintain the educational programme with the least possible disruption.

Outside help

The teacher's first task, then, must be to call in help, so that those who are qualified to do so can mount a programme to tackle the problem. This is likely to involve individual counselling, group therapy, special study assignments, a lasting contact with the home. The results will not emerge quickly, so the sooner a programme can be started, the better. The teacher will obviously wish to be kept informed of progress, and will give help wherever appropriate.

Meanwhile the teacher must do the best that is possible for the disruptive pupil within the constraints set by the normal classroom. It is an advantage if some kind of 'sanctuary' is available in the school to which the pupil can withdraw at times of great stress. This should not be portrayed as a punishment area, a 'sin bin', although it is difficult to prevent that interpretation being placed on it.

Behaviour modification techniques

The lesson by lesson handling of the disruptive pupil needs to be guided by the general tactics already discussed, but in a systematic and deliberate way. The idea of *teaching* good behaviour has developed in America into a school of thought, and there has been some acceptance that the teacher cannot hope to tackle underlying causes, but that good behaviour can nevertheless be taught. It is based on the learning theories of B. F. Skinner and the emphasis is on *systematic reinforcement*. Reinforcement is a regular technique of the teacher. Praise, good reports, gold stars, rewards, prizes, and privileges are all part of the technique, as are reprimands, withdrawal of privileges and punishments. Where the behaviour modification theories depart from current thinking in this country is their heavy reliance on the externally provided reinforcement as opposed to the inner understanding and motivation within the pupil. The argument is that, from the teacher's standpoint, the underlying causes of·the disruptive behaviour are beyond the reach of reason. So the emphasis needs to be a modification through *experience* rather than through reasoned argument.

135

Developing a programme for improving behaviour

Using these ideas as a general guide it might be possible for a teacher to devise a programme for a disruptive pupil somewhat on these lines.

1. Find out what rewards might be valued by the pupil. This will vary according to age and interests: praise, privileges, reports, material rewards, tokens.
2. Make specific agreements about behaviour over short periods of time, with a clear understanding about the rewards.
3. Do a formal check and, if the standard has been reached, make the award.
4. Try to arrange that the tasks that the pupil prefers and finds pleasing should follow and depend on tasks which are not preferred. The pleasant tasks are then seen as a reward for the completion of the unpleasant.
5. Try to arrange that the reinforcement techniques for the disruptive pupil should apply when he is working as a member of the group. The pressure of the whole group will be towards gaining the reward, and this may have a beneficial influence in the disruptive pupil.
6. Use negative reinforcement sparingly. Public reprimands are likely to be counter-productive.
7. Give attention to the pupil when behaviour is good, withhold when behaviour is bad. This is a counsel of perfection! The teacher simply cannot always ignore bad behaviour but there is a tendency to leave pupils alone when they are working well and only give them attention when they become a nuisance. The disturbed pupil wants attention, so it is obvious what he needs to do! The technique is to deal quickly, privately and unsympathetically with the bad behaviour, but to spend more time reviewing good work and behaviour, in a more public way and with a show of friendship. This is not easy to do, especially if one has developed classroom habits which are the very reverse.

Some teachers may react against the ideas of the behaviour modification school of thought. It has connotations of animal training, and it may fit rather uneasily within a normal classroom of thirty pupils. But it is worth taking the ideas on board, and trying them out in a limited way, remembering common sense and experience.

Summary

1. The behaviour of pupils in their classrooms has become a major cause of concern.

2. The causes of the problems can be traced to:
   - failures within society as a whole;
   - failures within the home;
   - failures within the schools;
   - the developmental problems of adolescence.
3. Classroom strategies. Long-term strategies which help a teacher to build a sound framework of disciplined behaviour are:
   - the teacher's knowledge and understanding including background knowledge and the specific knowledge about the pupils and their environment;
   - the teacher's state of preparedness, including the course materials, the classroom, the school rules, procedures, rewards, and punishments;
   - the teacher's personal image: knowledgeable, firm in purpose, resolute, caring.
4. Classroom tactics. Classroom life is complex and advice has to be tentative.
   - Design and establish good starting routines.
   - Establish a clear understanding about 'speaking' rules.
   - Develop routines for accomplishing regular organizational tasks.
   - Adopt a purely supervisory role at regular intervals throughout a lesson.
   - Use control actions as unobtrusively as possible.
   - Continue to demonstrate your 'knowledge'.
   - Maintain the momentum and smoothness of the lesson.
   - Anticipate discipline problems and act quickly and decisively.
   - Avoid confrontation.
5. The disruptive pupil. Special attention is required, with emphasis on:
   - the importance of outside help;
   - the use of behaviour modification techniques based on reinforcement theories.

Part Four

Implementing the programme

This section concentrates on the actual activities involved in the improvement of teaching. It relates to the model of teaching described in the last two sections. It emphasizes a systematic approach using subjective as well as objective methods. It assumes too that improvements can be best brought about by a combination of self-help and help from outside the school.

11. The improvement of classroom management

Classroom management is a set of tasks which are diverse and complex. The term includes much more than the layman's simplistic view of 'teaching'. It also includes much more than the techniques for controlling the behaviour of the class (a narrow interpretation which unfortunately some writers in America have used). It emphasizes the role of the teacher in the classroom as a manager, that is, a person who plans, coordinates, supervises, and evaluates the work while at the same time recognizing the importance of the human factors of motivation and self-development. It is worth quoting Peter Drucker, a leading management consultant and writer on management education: 'Being a manager, though, is more like being a parent, or a teacher.' Drucker had no illusions about the status of teaching!

The improvement of teaching (the word used in our enlarged sense) requires deliberate and purposeful action. It will not happen by wishing, or even make much progress by unsystematic and occasional 'drives'. It needs to be planned as a long-term, regular programme of activities which become part of the teacher's way of life.

It is best if it can be arranged on a team basis for the benefits of shared thinking, group planning, mutual aid, and mutual criticism are substantial. Ideally the team should be a functional team within the school organization, for example, a secondary school faculty or department, a primary school year team. If, for any reason, this is not possible, much can be accomplished by a small *ad hoc* team set up informally, for example, a team of two people, who have similar responsibilities, and who share a commitment to the improvement of their teaching, will be able to accomplish a great deal. To work entirely alone must be regarded as the last resort, but it is better to do that than to drift into complacency or defeatism.

It is best if the wish and the initiative come from the team members rather than being imposed from above. The team leader should see this as an opportunity to get every teacher involved in improvement work, rather than as an exercise in appraisal and in a paternalistic style of management. This means that the leader's own teaching must come under scrutiny, and be regarded as not necessarily any better than anybody else's. In fact, the wise team leader, knowing the threat that

141

many teachers perceive in work of this kind, will make sure that his leadership is by example rather than by precept. Nothing endears a leader to his followers more than the willingness to accept that in some important respects the leader is not the best performer. Andrew Carnegie's epitaph:

> Here lies a man
> Who knew how to enlist
> In his service
> Better men than himself.

It is best if the improvement of teaching can be supported by thinking, advice, and practical help from outside the team. This aid could come from within the school or from various external sources and it may come best after some experience has been acquired and some confidence built up. It is difficult to generalize, but where there is doubt and anxiety it may be wiser to make the work entirely internal for a start. On the other hand, where there is strong commitment and a willingness to experiment then the outsiders can make valuable contributions in the actual planning of the programme, and need to be involved at the outset.

The part played by the leader in the early stages will be a critical factor in the development of the programme. Creating awareness among the team members, building up interest and commitment requires management skills of a high order. The programme can easily appear as a threat, and it is the leader's job to build up confidence so that the rigorous and self-critical approach can be successfully adopted. Much should be done by example rather than by exhortation. The support and advice of people outside the team should be sought, but with a sensitive appreciation of the extent to which this might increase the sense of threat among the team members.

The Policy for Teaching

The Policy for Teaching, described in Chapter 3, must be the guide for a successful programme for the improvement of teaching. The ideal policy is one which has these characteristics:

- it enjoys the commitment of all the members of a team of teachers;
- it is based on systematic study of relevant literature;
- it responds to local conditions, policies, and developments;
- it has been produced as a team effort.

The ideal is not always possible, and it is better to have a policy, however inadequate it may seem, than no statement at all. Even one teacher working alone should make the effort to write out a personal statement about the characteristics of good teaching as they are currently perceived. To get started is the important thing (large oak trees and small acorns!).

The policy should be updated regularly, perhaps once a year. There are bound to be new influences, new pressures, new ideas, which need to be taken into account. And there are bound to be second thoughts about some of the items. They may not be sufficiently comprehensive, or well-balanced. They may have proved to be too impractical or even undesirable. The annual debate is good in its own right, because it focuses attention once again on this important matter, and will have the effect of re-charging the enthusiasm for positive action.

The current policy should occupy pride of place in the team's documentation. It should be displayed prominently, shown to visitors, given to newcomers. This means the design, typography, and finish should reflect the importance attached to it. Let us assume that we have a policy, written in the style described in Chapter 3. It will have ten major headings. Each heading is supported by a general statement of intent, and is followed by ten 'indicators' which can be used to help make judgements about the effectiveness of the teaching. In our example the ten headings were as follows:

1. The classroom
2. Planning and preparation
3. Resources
4. The teacher as leader and presenter
5. The pupil: motivation and needs
6. The classroom system
7. Personal relationships
8. The management of time
9. Management and control
10. Intellectual level

How does the individual make use of the policy? How do the members of the team cooperate to bring about improvements in their teaching? The remainder of this chapter describes an idealized programme of activities. It is capable of substantial modification to fit local conditions and needs.

A programme for the improvement of classroom management

The programme is described as a simple cycle of events. It is 'not so much a programme, more a way of life' and it can start modestly wherever the individual teacher is now. It aims to set up a perpetual motion of evaluation, objective setting, and action. It should result in an upward spiral of development, which is for the most part self-development. The idea of the cycle need not restrict thinking or planning. The teacher can join the cycle at any point. Steps can be emphasized, or skipped over lightly, or even omitted altogether. It can operate in the short-term, or in the long-term, or both. It can be used privately by one person, cooperatively by a small group of people, or it can be the occasion for joint action by a whole school or a group of schools.

The cycle described here assumes a small team working cooperatively on an annual programme. Although the programme is described as a sequence of separate steps, it would be more accurately imagined as a smooth sequence of activities. The steps merely help the explanation.

Step 1. Form the team and build up confidence

It is assumed that this will already have a clearly defined formation that will help cooperation. At the outset, the establishment of the right kinds of relationship is vital. The members must have a feeling of confidence in themselves and of trust in each other. It should be emphasized that the whole exercise is not concerned with appraisal or evaluation for purposes outside the professional concern of the team. This is self-development. It is going to start from where the teachers are now, and work to bring about improvements which are within their reach. It is not going to set impossible goals or to demand time and effort in totally unreasonable quantities. It must be seen as practical, realistic, worthwhile, and likely to enhance the social cohesion of the group.

Step 2. Devote time to the creation of a Policy for Teaching

This has already been thoroughly discussed and no more about the Policy itself need be stated here. It really does need time, because thorough research and reading are required, and also a lot of de-liberation. But this is not to say that the programme should be deferred, say for a year, while the policy is being prepared. It is far better to have a draft policy, put together as quickly as possible, as a starter. This means some experience in the steps of the whole programme can be gained while the revision and elaboration of the draft is taking place. The use of steps in explaining can have the unfortunate effect of suggesting that the programme is a tidy logical sequence. It is not, and should not be, like this. It is an untidy, practical business with means and ends both constantly under review and constantly influencing each other.

Step 3. The individual teacher evaluates his own teaching in the light of the Policy

In this step the question the teacher will ask himself over and over again is a simple one: 'Do the indicators in the Policy for Teaching describe what is actually happening in my classroom?' The question *is* a simple one, but the answers may not be easy to provide. However, it would not be right to pretend that teachers are incapable of judging their own strengths and weaknesses. In fact, where teachers are involved in, and committed to, this kind of activity their perceptions of their own performance can match very well with those of independent observers. Teachers often tend to be over critical of themselves.

A useful start might be to go through the Policy, marking each indicator with a personal assessment of its strength or weakness. A simple five-point scale works quite well.

4 = A particularly strong feature of my teaching
3 = A good feature of my teaching
2 = Not markedly strong or weak on this
1 = I am not satisfied about this
0 = I am a non-starter in this respect.

When this has been done a simple analysis might be attempted. An average can be calculated for each heading and possible clusters of related weaknesses or strengths might be identified. It might be possible for a purely descriptive account of one's teaching style to be developed from the analysis.

Before moving on to the next step many teachers will feel confident enough to ask for a second opinion. Here a colleague in the team, or even an outside observer, can be of great help. There need be no exact prescription for this but one way would be for the observer to spend time in the teacher's classroom with the object of doing an independent set of ratings based on the Policy for Teaching. The differences in perception will immediately be apparent and give rise to a stimulating discussion. Many observers, however, might feel unwilling to make these judgements after a relatively short period of observation. Or they may be teachers themselves without any hope of giving substantial amounts of time to the task, but nevertheless having a reasonable degree of familiarity with the teacher's work, picked up in an unstructured way over a long period of time. There is no reason why such a colleague should not adopt the role of counsellor, listening to the teacher's own analysis of strengths and weaknesses, asking questions for elucidation, seeking examples, pursuing arguments, challenging the reasoning. This

145

is how the debate should develop anyway, regardless of how it was initiated.

At the end of this stage the teacher should have a sense of having a profile of strengths and weaknesses, which can form the basis for the next move ahead.

Step 4. The teacher identifies key areas for improvement

At some stage in the discussion (whether it is a privately conducted one in the teacher's own head or an open discussion with a colleague) the teacher will become interested in one or more *key areas*. It may be that the evaluation has highlighted an aspect of his teaching about which he has been dissatisfied for some time. Or it may have revealed a specific weakness within an area in which the teacher felt himself to be particularly strong. Or during the discussion an interesting set of possibilities may have emerged. The focus on a key area is right at this stage and should be encouraged. Teaching can be best improved by driving spearheads into new territory and then gradually consolidating. It is hard to improve it by moving forward equally across the very wide front which the job represents but better to focus on just one key area at any one time. If the teacher is using a consultant, the selection of the key area should be discussed thoroughly. When the decision has been made, a period of inquiry and reflection is required. For the teacher this is a time for getting up to date with reading and if the key area has been drawn with tight boundaries this should not prove to be an impossible task. Here the use of an outsider can pay off, for example, a local authority adviser or college tutor can probably save the teacher many hours of search to get to the really useful and relevant texts.

Step 5. The teacher formulates specific objectives for improvement

The teacher now asks the question: 'What specific differences would I like to see in my classroom?' These must be within the key area already determined. It may be that an indicator in the Policy for Teaching will provide exactly what is required. Preferably the objective should:
- express behaviour or action on the part of the teacher or pupils;
- express behaviour that is observable.

This may take time to work out. First efforts tend to be vague and expressed in abstract language. More precision can be obtained by asking questions such as: 'How would an observer know that the desired changes had been brought about? What would the observer actually see?' The focus must always be on the results, on the achievements, not

146

on the processes by which these results are obtained. For example, if a teacher wanted to raise the intellectual level of the pupils' thinking, it would be more appropriate to express the objective in terms of pupil behaviour rather than teacher behaviour. At the end of the day someone may still have to make a subjective judgement as to whether what a pupil is saying, writing or doing represents a higher intellectual level than previously.

Step 6. The teacher works out a strategy for achieving each objective

We have to start by conceding that very often a teacher simply *does not know* how to achieve a particular objective. And there is no simple handbook of recipes which will help, the truth being that teaching does not yield to scientific analysis. There is still much of an art to it and achievement depends heavily on context and on personalities. Much of the improvement of teaching progresses by trial and error, and the best the teacher can do is to bring to bear all his knowledge and experience and propose a tentative solution. The fact that this may be little more than a bold conjecture need not be too worrying. The procedure is to subject the conjecture first to rigorous criticism. The teacher who is working with a colleague is again at an advantage because the debate which was started at the outset can proceed naturally at this point. After the proposed strategy has been thoroughly examined in terms of its logical consistency and its matching with experience, it is ready for the next stage.

Step 7. The teacher puts the strategy into practice

This sounds easy, but in fact it is not. Changing one's teaching styles and practices can be difficult. Lack of experience in the particular kind of activity may result in some incompetence showing itself. At this point many are ready to abandon the experiment and revert to the well-tried methods. 'It doesn't work—I've tried it.' Any teacher who attempts improvement on these lines must recognize that the new situation will almost certainly *generate incompetence*. So this becomes the personal testing time. The teacher needs to call on reserves of humility and persistence.

Again the teacher who has some support is at an advantage. A friendly colleague, occasionally observing, can help to refine the details of the strategy in practice. Attention needs to be given to *practical* details.

Step 8. The teacher collects information about changes which have taken place

Questions now must be asked to determine whether or not the objectives have been achieved. Can those precise behaviours and actions which were described in step 5 be observed now? What is the evidence? The teacher needs to record for his own satisfaction the actual events or the tangible evidence (like written work) which will lead to a warranted conclusion. The help of the observer colleague will be invaluable. It may be possible also to enlist the help of the pupils. A simple questionnaire or a class discussion may produce evidence which can be used.

Step 9. The teacher evaluates the whole cycle of events

The real value of this step is not so much to establish a case as for a court of law, but simply to provide a framework for a continuing discussion. It is necessary to review the objectives, to consider whether the strategies were right, to reflect on what happened in the classroom, to discuss and explore the significance of the events, and to come to conclusions about the whole cycle.

The cycle can and should be repeated. If the outcomes were unsatisfactory, better strategies might be devised next time. If the results were pleasing, it is likely that the teacher will wish to go on using the method. In subsequent cycles the chances of success will probably be greater as a result of experience. The important thing is to get started, however modestly.

A group approach

Many teachers may prefer to work throughout as a whole group, relying on group discussion as the principal driving force. Where the group shares a common teaching programme there is much to commend this approach.

Step 1. Form the team and build up confidence

As previously described (see p. 144).

Step 2. Devote time to the creation of a Policy for Teaching

As previously described (see p. 144).

Step 3. The group prepares an evaluation of the teaching by the whole group

Rather than focus on the individual the group collects a number of impressions about the style and quality of the teaching within the team as a whole. The use of the Policy for Teaching is the same as before, but the group can probably be more systematic in its use of outside help, and may think it useful at this stage to get the perceptions of the pupils. The statement which results is a *general* statement, and does not refer to specific teachers.

Step 4. The group identifies key areas for improvement

The principles are the same as those already described. The benefits for the group approach are the greater number of observations and insights which are available, and also the greater amount of support which can be arranged. It may be that improvements depend on a supply of different or additional resources. This can be more easily arranged by the group.

Step 5. The group discusses specific objectives for improvement and considers appropriate strategies

The group now becomes a forum for discussion rather than a decision-making body. Each teacher is allowed to formulate his own objectives and implement his own strategies. The group receives reports, acts in a counselling role, and maintains the interest and momentum.

Step 6. The group carries out an evaluation of the improvement work undertaken

The group relies heavily on the teachers' own reporting back, but pupil reports, and reports from independent observers, can also be helpful.

The two models described in this chapter can be varied to suit individual needs and circumstances. The message must be to get started and to gain experience as quickly as possible, so that more sophisticated methods of improving teaching can be developed.

Summary

1. The improvement of teaching is best when conducted as a group activity, well-planned, requiring the commitment of group members, and benefiting from outside help.

2. The Policy for Teaching is the guide for a successful programme of improvement.
3. A programme can be conducted by an individual teacher or by the whole group using a cycle which gives attention to:
   - team formation and confidence building;
   - the writing of the Policy for Teaching;
   - the evaluation of existing practice;
   - the identification of key areas for improvement;
   - the formulation of specific objectives;
   - the devising of new teaching strategies;
   - the implementation of the new strategies;
   - the evaluation of the new practices.

12. Classroom observation

Frequent reference was made in Chapter 11 to the support which the teacher could enjoy if a colleague or supporter from outside the school were able to observe lessons over a period of time. This chapter looks at ways of organizing this type of support.

In the last few years the teaching profession has become a little self-conscious about the apparent isolation of the teacher in the classroom. Although many teachers still regard any other adult persons in their classrooms as intruders, there is an increasing acceptance that isolation is harmful and not in the best interests of either pupils or teacher. Comparisons are made with other professions, where to observe and to be observed are regarded as an essential part of the initial training and subsequent development of the individual member. 'Opening up the classroom' has become a commonly expressed desire on the part of many teachers. The initial idea is often little more than a feeling that if teachers could only 'drift' in and out of each other's classrooms a lot of knowledge about each other's styles and methods would be picked up, casually and almost accidentally. The idea seems attractive and not potentially threatening.

Thinking has moved beyond the stage where teachers have acquired a more determined attitude to self-improvement, and this has been helped by the creation of special posts in schools with responsibilities for staff development. Many of these 'professional tutors' or 'staff tutors' have developed an interest in more systematic forms of classroom observation.

It comes as a surprise to many teachers, therefore, that classroom observation is a well-developed research technique and that there is a vast literature on the subject. Although most of the work has been done in the last twenty years, the origins can be traced back to the early years of the century. Virtually all of the work has been done by researchers, with research objectives in mind, but increasingly teacher-training has come under the influence of the systematic classroom observation techniques. Can these techniques and instruments developed for research purposes be used or adapted for use by teachers themselves? Is it conceivable that we might develop a 'scientific' way of improving teaching through the use of systematic observation? How easy or difficult is it for teachers to devise their own observation instruments and methods? These, and a number of related questions, must now be tackled.

Systematic classroom observation

The first problem facing an observer in a classroom is the complexity: so many different things are happening at the same time. Even in a class teaching situation each individual pupil is acting independently, for example, one may be listening to the teacher, another writing, another day-dreaming, and so on. In a situation organized for individual or group learning the classroom offers even greater diversity. So the first requirement for the classroom observer is to define *what* it is that he is preparing to observe and *who* is the target of his observation. In research work these decisions are significant, because in the choices that he is forced to make the researcher has to reveal a theoretical standpoint.

Who is to be observed?

Some of the instruments developed for classroom observation have focused entirely on the teacher while others have focused entirely on one child. In each of these it is possible to produce a detailed blow-by-blow account of a lesson, but at the expense of all other information. By careful sampling techniques it is possible to get more limited information across a wider population in the room. The choice is a difficult one because compromise and sacrifice have to be accepted. This problem highlights the need for the observer to be absolutely clear about the purposes of the observation.

What is to be observed?

This is an even bigger problem! Is the observer looking at the teacher's personal attributes as a teacher, or at specific actions, or at global strategies? Is the observer wishing to record what they say? Is it the intellectual content of the lesson which interests him, or is it the organization of the lesson and the routine procedures? Is it the way the classroom itself is laid out? Is it the way that pupils are interacting with the teacher, or with each other? The questions could be endless, therefore the observer must determine what is the *focus* of his interest?

Two American researchers have compiled an enormous collection of classroom observation instruments (Simon and Boyar, 1970) in which they distinguish seven areas that have been used by researchers:

- affective
- cognitive
- psychomotor
- activity

- procedures and routines
- sociological structure
- physical environment

The affective area

This area is concerned with the emotional aspect of classroom life. Some of the instruments set out to measure the amount of support or non-support in the teacher's style. Others focus on the extent to which the teacher's actions are orientated towards understanding the pupil's attitudes and feelings, or towards making judgements about them.

The cognitive area

This area is concerned with the intellectual life of the classroom. In the instruments that focus on this area, the researchers try to identify different kinds of intellectual activity:

- data recall: the simplest form;
- data processing: handling data, classifying, defining it, analysing, and making inferences from it;
- evaluation: making judgements using different criteria.

This also covers all the different uses of language in the classroom, and many systems are concerned with the recording and analysis of language.

The psychomotor area

This is concerned with such matters as getting ready to work and carrying out the various administrative routines that may be required. Some instruments focus on the distinction between activities that are related to the content of the lesson, and those that are not. The sociological structure area is concerned with the roles, status, and interactions of all the participants in the lesson.

The physical environment area

Within this area, the classroom itself, the furniture and equipment, and the learning resources are included. The way that the members of the class interact with the environment is also included.

Categories for observation

Having determined the focus of the observation, the observer has still a substantial area to observe. He needs to break it down still further into a number of categories, each defining an event, an activity, a verbal exchange, which *can be observed*. The category system he devises must satisfy two important tests:

- it must cover the whole area selected for observation;
- each category must be capable of clear definition and must not overlap with any other.

In practice, any system which could satisfy these two tests to perfection would have to be so simple as to be worthless. As ambition increases, the second test becomes increasingly difficult to satisfy. The designer of the instrument will have to spend more effort on the definition of his categories in order to help the user.

Designing a category system is an interesting exercise in its own right. Readers will no doubt recognize the similarity between the Policy for Teaching breakdown and the classroom observation categories.

Policy for Teaching		*Classroom Observation*
Major heading	=	Major focus
Indicators	=	Observation categories

Armed with a category system the researcher is now ready to plan the actual observation. Two more things need to be resolved first:

- How are the data to be recorded?
- What are the units of measurement?

Data recording

The live observer is not the only method. There has been much experimentation with audio and video technology in order to provide a full record of aspects of a lesson for later analysis at leisure.

The video recording gives a visual and sound record which can be analysed by playing back several times. If it is done with technical sophistication the results can be very informative. The main weakness is that good quality recording requires a lot of equipment and a lot of care; and all this tends to produce an unreal atmosphere in the classroom.

The sound recording can be done much less obtrusively, particularly if a radiomicrophone is used by the teacher. This will give a continuous record of all the verbal exchanges in which the teacher is involved. Recording the whole class, and pupil–pupil exchanges, are much more difficult.

Coding systems

How exactly does the observer (whether observing live or recorded) actually record the events or activities which constitute his category system? There are a number of options.

- Category change: the observer simply notes when a new activity starts.
- Time unit: the observer makes a record at a fixed time interval, e.g., every three seconds he decides which category represents the events now taking place, and notes it accordingly.
- Topic or content change: the observer notes the new topic.
- Speaker change: the observer notes who the new speaker is.
- Time sample: the observer records all the codable events in a fixed time period.

Clearly the coding system needs to be matched to the chosen category system. It is hoped that the examples of observation systems that follow will make this clear.

Subsequent analysis

The raw data from the classroom will subsequently have to be analysed. The designer of an observation instrument usually prepares printed checklists for observers to use so that totals and patterns may easily be perceived at the analysis stage.

The Flanders interaction analysis

This is the best known of the classroom observation instruments. It has been widely used and modified, and subjected to much learned debate. It can lead to a very sophisticated analysis of classroom activity, and it can also be used in a simple way. The description that follows is not intended to serve as a primer for the use of the system but as an illustration of a widely used system. Readers who wish to experiment with it are advised to consult the literature listed in the bibliography.

Purposes of the system

The system focuses on the interaction between individuals in the classroom setting. It is most interested in the analysis of *initiative* and *response*: who makes the first move; who is leading and who is following; where do the ideas come from, and how are they responded to. It is a system based entirely on classroom talk. For the most part it seems to assume that the teacher will always be relating to the whole class, and difficulties arise when the observed classes are organized on an

155

individual or small-group basis. It does not fit neatly into any one of Simon and Boyar's areas; it covers parts of the affective area, but it is also concerned with cognitive matters. Nevertheless, this is a well-defined system in its own terms and deals with an important aspect of teaching.

The categories for observation

Table 12.1 shows the ten categories of the system. The three main headings: teacher talk, pupil talk, silence or confusion clearly cover all possibilities.

Table 12.1 *Flanders' Interaction Categories* (FIAC)*

	Response	1. *Accepts feeling* Accepts and clarifies an attitude for the feeling tone of a pupil in a non-threatening manner. Feelings may be positive or negative. Predicting and recalling feelings are included.
		2. *Praises or encourages* Praises or encourages pupil action or behaviour. Jokes that release tension, but not at the expense of another individual; nodding head, or saying 'Um-hm?' or 'go on' are included.
		3. *Accepts or uses ideas of pupils* Clarifying, building, or developing ideas suggested by a pupil. Teacher extensions of pupil ideas are included but as the teacher brings more of his own ideas into play, shift to category five.
Teacher talk		4. *Asks questions* Asking a question about content or procedure, based on teacher ideas, with the intent that a pupil will answer.
	Initiation	5. *Lecturing* Giving facts or opinions about content or procedures; expressing *his own* ideas, giving *his own* explanation, or citing an authority other than a pupil.
		6. *Giving directions* Directions, commands, or orders to which a pupil is expected to comply.
		7. *Criticizing or justifying authority* Statements intended to change pupil behaviour from non-acceptable to acceptable pattern; bawling someone out; stating why the teacher is doing what he is doing; extreme self-reference.

Pupil talk	Response	8.	*Pupil-talk—response* Talk by pupils in response to teacher. Teacher initiates the contact or solicits pupil statement or structures the situation. Freedom to express own ideas is limited.
	Initiation	9.	*Pupil-talk—initiation* Talk by pupils which they initiate. Expressing own ideas; initiating a new topic; freedom to develop opinions and a line of thought, like asking thoughtful questions; going beyond the existing structure.
Silence		10.	*Silence or confusion* Pauses, short periods of silence and periods of confusion in which communication cannot be understood by the observer.

*No scale is implied by these numbers. Each number is classificatory; it designates a particular kind of communication event. To write these numbers down during observation is to enumerate, not to judge a position on a scale.

The problems come in trying to make distinctions between adjacent categories. Here it becomes necessary for researchers to consult the handbooks and to undergo systematic training in order to achieve a high level of reliability.

The coding procedures

From a convenient position in the classroom, the observer simply writes down every three seconds the category number of the verbal exchange which is just taking place. At the end of his period of observation he simply has a long string of numbers. Flanders emphasizes that a steady tempo is more important than the actual interval (which is purely arbitrary).

Some observers find it helpful to use a grid paper, 20 columns by 30 lines. Each line then represents a minute, and the whole represents a half-hour observation. This can help in establishing a steady rhythm. At the end of half an hour's observation the observer will have nothing more than 600 numbers.

Presenting the results

By themselves, 600 numbers are meaningless. A system of presentation is required before analysis and discussion can take place. A useful method of presentation can be achieved by *pairing* the events. Since one event in the classroom often follows as a result of the previous event, this offers some useful information. Thus a sequence of numbers is now treated as a sequence of pairs.

  2   4   8   5   6   4   8 would become

    2–4   4–8   8–5   5–6   6–4   4–8

Note that apart from the first and last numbers each number now appears twice.

The pairs are presented in a 10×10 matrix: the first number in the pair is used as the line number; the second is the column number. Each pair is shown as a tally mark. Fig. 12.1 shows the start of a matrix using the above numbers.

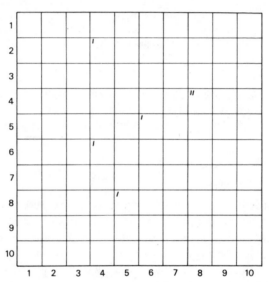

Fig. 12.1 *Matrix representation of classroom observation*

Analysis and discussion

When a matrix has been completed for an episode in a lesson or for a whole lesson, it is a very rich source of information and speculation. The interpretation of the matrix is too big a subject to develop here, but the following thoughts might stimulate further investigation of the system.

    4–4–4   sustained questioning by the teacher.

    4–8–4–8   short questions and short answers.

    3–9–9–3–3–9–9   a dialogue in which teacher and pupils use each other's ideas.

    5–5–5–6–5–5–4   a teacher-dominated period.

It is possible using the matrix to work out:
- How much variety was there in the lesson?
- What proportion of the talking was done by the teacher?
- How did the pupils respond to the teacher's talk?
- How did the teacher respond to the pupils' talk?
- Did the teacher respond at all in an affective way?

The Flanders system is an interesting example of a well-developed approach to classroom observation. It is easy to use in a simple way, and yet is capable of generating thought and can encourage teachers to extend the range of their classroom strategies. Of course, there are many aspects of classroom life which it does not touch, particularly where individual and small-group methods are being used.

The ORACLE project

ORACLE (Observational Research and Classroom Learning Evaluation) was a large-scale observational study of primary school classrooms in this country (1975–80). It is interesting, not only for its findings, but also for its observation techniques which seem particularly appropriate for the modern classroom where the emphasis is on variety of activity.

Purposes of the project

The major objective of the project was 'to study the relative effectiveness of different teaching approaches across the main subject areas of primary school teaching'. This was to be accomplished through systematic observation. This would enable the team to describe 'the richness and variety of what goes on in the modern primary classroom', and to study the effect of these patterns on the progress of the pupils.

The observation instruments are more complex than the Flanders instrument. They represent an attempt to cover the events and activities on a very broad front. It follows that they are more difficult to administer in a consistently reliable way.

All the observers on the project were experienced teachers and all received two weeks' full-time training. Nevertheless, the instruments are of great interest; the category system and the definitions will stimulate thinking for those who wish to study the behaviour of individual children and to evaluate their own classroom practice.

The categories for observation

Two observation schedules were used, one focused on the pupils, the other on the teachers.

Table 12.2 *The observation categories of the Pupil Record*

Category	Item	Brief definition of item
Coding the pupil–adult categories		
1. Target's role	INIT	Target attempts to become focus of attention (not focus at previous signal)
	STAR	Target is focus of attention
	PART	Target in audience (no child is focus)
	LSWT	Target in audience (another child is focus)
2. Interacting adult	TCHR	Target interacts with teacher
	OBSR	Target interacts with observer
	OTHER	Target interacts with any other adult such as the head or secretary
3. Adult's interaction	TK WK	Adult interacts about task work (task content or supervision)
	ROUTINE	Adult interacts about routine matter (classroom management and control)
	POS	Adult reacts positively to task work (praises)
	NEG	Adult reacts negatively to behaviour, etc. (criticizes)
	IGN	Adult ignores attempted initiation
4. Adult's communication setting	IND ATT	Adult gives private attention to to target pupil
	GROUP	Adult gives private attention to target's group
	CLASS	Adult interacts with whole class
	OTHER	Adult gives private attention to another child or group or does not interact
Coding the pupil–pupil categories		
5. Target's role	BGNS	Target successfully begins a new contact
	COOP	Target cooperates by responding to an initiation
	TRIES	Target unsuccessfully tries to initiate
	IGN	Target ignores attempted initiation
	SUST	Target sustains interaction

Category	Item	Brief definition of item
6. Mode of interaction	MTL	Non-verbal, mediated solely by materials
	CNTC	Non-verbal, mediated by physical contact or gesture (with or without materials
	VRB	Verbal (with or without materials, physical contact or gesture)
7a. Task of other pupil(s)	S TK	Same as target's task
	D TK	Different to target's task
7b. Sex and number of other pupil(s)	SS	Target interacts privately with one pupil of same sex
	OS	Target interacts with one pupil of opposite sex
	SEV SS	Target interacts with two or more pupils having same sex as target
	SEV OS	Target interacts publicly with two or more pupils, of whom one at least is of the opposite sex to the target
7c. Base of other pupil(s)	OWN BS	From target's own base
	OTH BS	From another base

Coding the activity and location categories

8. Target's activity	COOP TK	Fully involved and cooperating on approved task work (e.g., reading)
	COOP R	Fully involved and cooperating on approved routine work (e.g., sharpening a pencil)
	DSTR	Non-involved and totally distracted from all work by the observer
	DSTR OBSR	Non-involved and totally distracted from all work by the observer
	DSRP	Non-involved and aggressively disrupting work of other pupil(s)
	HPLY	Non-involved and engaging in horseplay with other pupil(s)
	WAIT TCHR	Waiting to interact with the teacher
	CODS	Partially cooperating and partially distracted from approved work
	INT TCHR	Interested in teacher's activity or private interaction with other pupil(s)
	INT PUP	Interested in the work of other pupil(s)
	WOA	Working on an alternative activity which is not approved work
	RIS	Not coded because the pupil is responding to internal stimuli

161

Table 12.2 — *continued*

Category	Item	Brief definition of item
	NOT OBS	Not coded because the target is not observed for some reason
	NOT LIST	Not coded because the target's activity is not listed
9. Target's location	P IN	Target in base
	P OUT	Target out of base but not mobile
	P MOB	Target out of base and mobile
	P OUT RM	Target out of room
10. Teacher activity and location	T PRES	Teacher present with target through interaction or physical proximity
	T ELSE	Teacher privately interacting elsewhere with other pupil(s) or visitor
	T MNTR	Teacher not interacting but monitoring classroom activities
	T HSKP	Teacher not interacting but housekeeping
	T OUT RM	Teacher out of room

Only one pupil at a time was the target for the observation. The target pupil's behaviour was coded at regular twenty-five-second intervals. At each interval a number of entries had to be made in order to provide a full record of the pupil's actions.

Table 12.3 *The observation categories of the teacher record*

Conversation		Silence
Questions		*Silent interaction*
Task		Gesturing
Q1	recalling facts	Showing
Q2	offering ideas, solutions (closed)	Marking
Q3	offering ideas, solutions (open)	Waiting
Task Supervision		Story
Q4	referring to task supervision	Reading
Routine		Not observed
Q5	referring to routine matter	Not coded
Statements		*No interaction*
Task		Adult interaction
S1	of facts	Visiting pupil
S2	of ideas, problems	Not interacting
Task supervision		Out of room
S3	telling child what to do	

Conversation		Silence
S4	praising work or effort	Audience
S5	feedback on work or effort	Composition
Routine		Activity
S6	providing information, directions	
S7	providing feedback	
S8	of critical control	
S9	of small talk	

The *silent interaction* categories were included to indicate when the teacher was *gesturing*, *showing* by writing or demonstrating on the blackboard, *marking* pupils' work in their presence, *waiting* for the class to settle, reading a *story* to the class or listening to a pupil *reading* aloud. To deal with cases where the observer had difficulty in recording the activity two further categories, *not observed* and *not coded*, were available. If the latter was used the observers wrote a brief description of the event in a 'Notes' box so that a decision as to the correct classification could be made later. If no *interaction* was taking place one of the four categories under this heading was coded covering such situations as visits from teachers and parents or pupils from other classes (*adult interaction* or *visiting pupil*), *not interacting* while silently monitoring, housekeeping or going *out of room* for some purpose or other. The observer also coded the type of the teacher's *audience* (class, group, or individual pupil), its *composition* in terms of the number of target pupils, if any, present, and the curricular *activity* of the child or children with whom the teacher was interacting.

The teacher's record was designed to be used in a similar way; in this the observer had to classify the teacher's conversation or the nature of the silent interaction taking place.

The coding procedures

Each observer worked to a carefully planned timetable involving the observation of eight individual pupils and the teacher. Some interesting features of this were:

- six observation sessions were carried out per term;
- each session devoted $4\frac{1}{2}$ minutes to each of the eight pupils and 10 minutes to the teacher;
- the timetable was so arranged that individual pupils would be observed at different times in the day;
- the sample of pupils was arranged to provide two high achievers, two low achievers, and four from a middle group (equal boys and girls in each case);
- the observers did not know the achievement category of their target pupils; the teacher did not know the names of the target pupils.

Other evidence used

The observers also collected other information during their periods in the schools in order to fill out the record of classroom observations. These included details like seating arrangements, an outline of the curricular activities, the forms of organization, the materials used, and a daily timetable. The observer also wrote a descriptive account of the work of the teacher to try to capture those aspects of classroom life which might not be adequately covered by an observation schedule. Finally, there was a teacher questionnaire at the end of the whole period of observation.

Analysis and discussion

The observations carried out by the ORACLE team have been the subject of a thorough analysis. They were carried out with great care and provided a mass of objective data. The project has been an inspiration to all those who are concerned with the improvement of teaching. It is not possible here to examine the findings of the team, but interested teachers, secondary as well as primary, will find the project reports well worth studying (see Galton, Simon and Croll (1980) and Galton and Simon (1980)).

School-based classroom observation

Classroom observation should become part of the way of life in our schools. However, since it takes up time, it will have to be justified in competition with many other pressures. Teachers cannot hope to investigate with the thoroughness of a full-time research project but they can learn a lot from a study of the work of these projects.

Teacher's classroom observations

A number of practical suggestions follow.

Be determined to start as soon as possible
There is always the temptation to put off a new venture. The conditions never seem completely favourable, probably they never will be, so it is worth getting started. A little experience gives confidence.

Make the observation an integral part of a programme for the improvement of teaching
Everything that we have said about the involvement of the teachers and the careful thinking about styles and methods applies with great force in classroom observation.

Use a cooperative approach
The simple partnership can be quickly established and brought into operation. If the members are colleagues and friends there is likely to be little difficulty. Think of the exercise as one of mutual aid.

Avoid a one-way arrangement with the superior observing the subordinate
This is threatening and it will be counter-productive in terms of the improvements which are sought. It is another matter, of course, if a team leader succeeds in building up a trusting relationship. This is usually done by the leader being the first to be observed.

Regard all data and all discussions which stem from the observations as absolutely confidential
To do otherwise would be to misunderstand the whole purpose of the exercise.

Start modestly and be specific
It is difficult to design a complex observation schedule. It is also difficult to carry out observations using complex instruments like the ORACLE teacher and pupil records. At the beginning, it is far better to identify one possible small area of improvement, and to plan an observation round it.

Do not be afraid of observing for practical details
Many of the suggestions made in previous chapters of this book are essentially about practical details. They are worth studying through classroom observation.

Do not intervene in any way during a period of classroom observation

Cooperate with other groups and partnerships to exchange experiences and to swap 'tools'
The 'tools' are the forms which have been designed to help the observer

in his tasks. They are often produced on squared paper, each cell usually representing a unit of time.

Remember the importance of feedback

The observation itself is only a means to an end. The observer must report back. The data which he has collected is the start of a constructive discussion. It is not the place of the observer to adopt the role of expert counsellor, but to keep to his humbler role of just an additional pair of eyes and ears, and a readiness to listen and to talk.

Observing is part of the learning process

The opportunity to observe must be viewed as learning experience in itself. When classroom observation is taking place *two* teachers are likely to benefit.

Summary

1. Systematic observation addresses itself to a complex situation.
2. Seven areas of investigation have been identified:
   - affective
   - cognitive
   - psychomotor
   - activity
   - procedures and routines
   - sociological structures
   - physical environment.
3. The classroom observer uses:
   - a category system
   - a coding system
   - a system for presenting and analysing data.
4. The Flanders Interactive Analyses is a well-tried system concerned with interactions between individuals in the classroom, particularly with regard to initiative and response.

   The matrix form for presentation of data lends itself to sophisticated analysis. It is a stimulating system which encourages teachers to extend the range of their classroom strategies.
5. The ORACLE Project is an example of a large-scale study of schools based on observation techniques. The Pupils' Record and the Teacher's Record are particularly suitable for the modern classroom with its rich and varied pattern of activities. In addition to a sophisticated analysis of the observed data the project also relied heavily on description accounts prepared by the observers.

6. School-based classroom observation. Teachers should organize their own observations as part of a general programme for the improvement of teaching. The approach should be cooperative and practical. The programme should start modestly, focusing on specific improvements.

13. Using outside help

Our emphasis so far has been on self-help, and this is a practical and realistic outlook. The people who can help teachers in the improvement of their work are thin on the ground, and it would be unwise to expect too much or to be too dependent.

The case for using outside help is overwhelming. The outsider often *starts fresh*. He may be quite new to the school and will not be burdened by past experience or accumulated prejudice. He will have the benefit of *perspective*, able to see problems as part of the whole, and able to compare them with situations elsewhere. Provided he is a wise and well-balanced person he stands a good chance of being fairly objective in his judgements. He will have the benefit of *independence*; since he is not part of the school's organization, he will be able to express his views without fear or favour. He may well possess *expertise* which the school may be able to use for its benefit and he may have knowledge of or access to *resources* which will help the school in its tasks. These benefits have to be set against the disadvantages. Because he does not know the school he may make unwise judgements and be the cause of conflict. He may not be willing to help in a practical way and to have his ideas tested in practice, only to advise and withdraw, leaving implementation problems to the teacher.

Generally, the advantages of using outside help outweigh the disadvantages. The teacher's job is to maximize the advantages and minimize the disadvantages.

Who is available?

Local Authority advisers

In spite of some recent cuts most local authorities have a staff of advisers of whom many are employed as subject specialists or 'stage' (e.g., primary school) specialists. Teachers often have high expectations of their advisers and are often disappointed, for the following reasons:

- Advisers are few in number, almost invariably inadequate for the number of schools.
- Advisers have heavy demands made on them by their local authority.
- There is a trend (supported by many of the advisers themselves)

away from advising and helping individual teachers and towards evaluative and administrative roles.

The situation varies enormously between authorities and even within authorities. The only useful generalization is that where an adviser is able and willing to help in a programme for the improvement of teaching, the chances are that he will bring all the outsider advantages listed above and few, if any, of the disadvantages.

Teachers' centre wardens

Increasingly, wardens have taken more significant roles in in-service education, and many are in a strong position to be of real practical help. Some authorities really believe that the centres are *teachers'* centres, and the control of the centre programme is very much in the hands of the teachers. Where this is so, support for a programme of improvement can be powerful, particularly as regards the coordination of outside help.

Local support services

These include services like the schools' library, museum, audio-visual, and art services as well as centres specifically geared towards particular school subjects. These 'on demand' services are sources of great strength, although they are not likely to be directly involved in the actual programme of improvement itself.

Local development projects

Where these exist, they can be nearest to the ideal support for the improvement of teaching. Often they are working to a specific brief, for example, independent learning; gifted children; slow-learning children. They are usually staffed by experienced teachers who are able to concentrate their efforts acting as consultants and helpers.

Colleges and University Departments of Education

These are a rich source of possibilities. Most mount their own programme of short and long courses. In addition many will respond to requests from individual schools for school-based courses on consultancy. Some offer short-term 'attachments' to enable individual teachers to carry out a specific investigation with tutorial help. An 'in-service coordinator' or 'further professional studies tutor' is usually the first contact for the interested teacher. In addition many university and college staff are pursuing their own research, and are often eager to contact teachers who share their interests.

Major research projects

These are usually under the control of a University or the National Foundation for Educational Research. Involvement in one of these usually has a beneficial spin-off for a school, and makes it well worth the extra time and effort required.

The Schools Council

The Schools Council is the main national body concerned with development work in curriculum and teaching methods. Its work is currently organized in four main programmes for a three-year period from 1980 to 1983. Each programme covers a wide range of activities, including small-scale research, conferences, the development of teaching materials and case studies of good practice. Two of the programmes (programme two and programme four) are particularly relevant to the improvement of teaching.

Programme two: helping individual teachers to become more effective

Topics of interest include teacher–pupil interaction, diagnostic assessment, profile reporting, teacher self-evaluation.

Programme four: individual pupils

This programme is concentrating on the individualization of learning opportunities for children with special educational needs: because of some physical or mental handicap; disruptive pupils; members of ethnic minority groups; and gifted pupils.

The Council wishes to involve teachers as much as possible, and communicates through an efficient service:
- a team of regional field officers who support the work of teachers' centres and curriculum development in schools;
- regional information centres in Cardiff, Newcastle, and Wakefield;
- a frequently updated *Project Profiles* which gives detailed information about the work of the individual projects;
- a termly newsletter called *Schools' Council News*.

What kinds of support can they offer?

Courses

We can distinguish between long courses, short courses, and school-focused courses.

The long course is usually an award-bearing course. It is set up by a college or university and tends to emphasize theory, research, and subject disciplines. Its aims are the personal and professional development of the individual teachers. It relies mainly on the lecture/tutorial/discussion methods. The value of the long course is its intellectual vigour. It does not bear directly on the issues involved in the improvement of teaching, but it can rightly claim to establish the intellectual base from which most new ideas and initiatives will spring.

The short course is usually much more orientated to the practical concerns of the teacher. It is often organized on workshop style. But like the long course it is usually at a centre away from the school, involves individual teachers from different schools, relies heavily on non-teachers for its leadership, and rarely provides any follow-up activities after the course. For these reasons the short course has come in for much criticism. It is claimed that short courses generally fail to make a difference to the work of the schools. There is no fundamental reason why this should be so. There is perhaps a need for fewer short courses with more expected both from the leaders and the participants in terms of preparation, involvement, and follow-up.

The school-focused course is markedly different. It usually takes place at the school, is concerned with the perceived needs of the school, is often specific to the job that the teachers are actually doing now, and is essentially practical in outlook. Its great strength is its built-in assumptions about follow-up; the course members are also the executive team of the school. A possible weakness is that the school itself may not *always* be the best judge of its own needs, and may lack the knowledge and 'know-how' for successful in-service work. The programme may lack sufficient stimulus from outside. These are the dangers, but where school-focused work is well done it can, by skilfully blending internal perceptions and knowledge with outside expertise and advice, produce remarkably good results.

Resources support

We can distinguish between organizations which make resources, those which loan them, and those which provide a reference collection. Many

171

local organizations are involved in all three. For example, many teachers' centres aim to make available reprographic and studio facilities to support cooperative resource making, or even to provide an on-demand service for individual teachers. They also organize loans of curriculum materials and audio-visual resources, and provide a permanent reference collection of project materials, research reports and periodicals.

Many of the resources organizations are specialized. Schools' library services maintain reference collections, but tend to concentrate on their loan services to schools, both fiction and non-fiction. Well-chosen collections of non-fiction resources are particularly valued by the schools. Schools' museum services emphasize their permanent exhibitions but often support these by curricular materials for use in association with a museum visit, and many organize highly efficient loan services. Schools art services operate on similar lines, and can help the quality of teaching far beyond the confines of a school art and crafts department.

In some areas, centres specializing entirely in resource-making have been established. Methods of working vary. Some endeavour to respond to each and every request which comes from a school. Others work more like development projects, working with teachers to identify common needs, and then concentrating on the development of a coherent collection of resources to respond to those needs.

Research projects

On the face of it, research projects are not set up to help individual schools. They aim to make generalized statements as a result of systematic investigation in a number of schools. But there is often much benefit for the individual participating school. Researchers today are much less clinical in their approach. They become 'participant observers', as much interested in the viewpoints, reactions and experiences of the teachers as in their own observations and data. They try to strike the delicate balance between staying aloof and getting personally involved. This can be interesting for the school concerned; the researcher becomes in many senses a consultant to the school.

Consultancy

This term is being used more frequently to express the idea that a school can most effectively use outside help when that help is concentrated and sustained, and when the control of the arrangement is in the hands of the school. The growth of the idea has also come about as a result of the declining number of new entrants to initial training, and the consequent redeployment of college staff towards in-service education.

The style is not new for the work of many advisory teachers in specialist centres has often been of a consultancy type. Such centres as remedial centres, reading centres, multicultural centres, specialist subject centres, centres for gifted children, have all encouraged the idea of a sustained period of support in one school or even with one teacher.

The consultancy model, in its ideal form, is represented by a process which starts with the identification of a problem or a need, and then follows through a cycle of building up relationships, diagnosis, exploration of alternative approaches, trial and error, and a final stage at which the improvements are stabilized. It is an exciting prospect, but sadly, there is an acute shortage of people who have available the required combination of resources, time, and expertise.

How can teachers make the most of outside help?

Much of a teacher's time and energy are spent on matters internal to the school, for example, keeping things going, negotiating, and communicating with colleagues, handling the constant stream of needs and problems which the pupils create. It is not surprising that the habit of looking outwards is not as strongly developed as it might be. Yet the need to do so is vital. Schools need to change, to look at better ways of doing things, to discover new opportunities, to realize that new solutions are available to solve old problems. The school that is turned in on itself is going to miss a lot of stimulus and a lot of information. Although it may seem that internal thinking and internally generated solutions can be the best informed, there are the permanent dangers of myopia, tunnel vision, and complacency.

Because the pressures which force a school to turn in on itself are so great, it is necessary to create counter pressures. Teachers who believe in looking outwards must be determined in their intention, deliberate and systematic in their approach, persistent in the face of difficulties.

Acquire as much knowledge as possible

Knowledge of people, institutions, activities, developments is the first requirement. Some of it can be achieved through official documentation such as:

- prospectuses of institutions;
- lists of publications (e.g., research bodies, development organizations);

173

- published handbooks (e.g., the *Education Yearbook*);
- local authority handbooks.

Much can be achieved through membership of professional organizations:

- teachers' unions;
- professional subject associations;
- specialist interest societies.

Much knowledge comes from reading, particularly periodicals which are up to date and often focus on the work of individual practitioners. But most knowledge comes from personal contact, through attendance on courses or at conferences, through local meetings, and simply through the 'grapevine'. Knowledge is a thing which can soon grow of its own accord. One contact invariably leads to another; one source of information opens up new sources beyond. Energy to pursue the leads seems to be the main attribute of success.

Build up relationships

It would be wrong to take this for granted. Teachers may be wary of outsiders, but they should also recognize the anxieties and uncertainties which the outsider has about the school. Teachers are often perceived as being hostile to non-teachers regardless of individual merits ('When did *he* last do some teaching?'); as being dogmatic ('It wouldn't work with my kids.'); and as impatient for practical results ('Why doesn't he tell us exactly what to do?'). It is best to work on the assumption that relationships need to be built up carefully, and what is more, serviced regularly.

It is worth while at the outset to try to know as much as possible about the outsider and his background and present job. There may be some points of contact which will help to establish friendliness and a feeling of familiarity. The outsider needs to be welcomed not only in the sense of normal courtesies, but also to be given the feeling that the school is eager to share its ambitions and problems and is ready to engage in a constructive dialogue. The process of building the relationship is under way.

Before trying to define the ultimate goals of this endeavour we must look at some possible causes of friction:

- make sure that other colleagues are not undermining your efforts by displaying indifference or even hostility to the outsider;
- make sure that the outsider is not 'using' the school for his own purposes;

- make sure that the outsider is not already.committed ideologically to a particular kind of solution;
- make sure that he is prepared to see it through.

At least, these things should be uncovered. They may, or may not, be sufficient reason for calling off the cooperation. There is nothing wrong, for example, in an outsider collecting data for a piece of research or a book, provided all the normal safeguards and courtesies are assured, and provided the activity really represents what the school wants.

Ideally the relationship, as it develops, should show at least some evidence of the following:

- open minds: a willingness to listen on both sides, a feeling of give and take in discussion, a readiness to defer decisions;
- mutual support: a readiness to share information and ideas, and to help overcome problems and difficulties;
- honesty: so that differences are registered quickly, but sincerely and without threat, before positions get too set.

Cooperate in a systematic way

Four stages are suggested in the life of a cooperative consultancy:

- examining the problems;
- examining possible solutions;
- gaining acceptance of the chosen solution;
- establishing the new arrangements.

First, time has to be spent looking at the problems or opportunities which have given rise to the consultancy. It is necessary to examine them very thoroughly and to set them in their context. What seems to be a problem may be only a surface manifestation of an underlying malaise. Teachers must be ready at this stage to open up the sources of information and opinion. The consultant must be given free access so that he can not only get a clear understanding about needs, but also so that he can begin to formulate some possible solutions through knowledge of resources, people, obstacles, strengths, and weaknesses. Maximum participation by as many teachers as possible is highly desirable at this stage. Time spent simply describing problems is not time wasted, because 'knowing the right questions to ask' is often half the battle!

Second, a range of alternative solutions should be examined. The consultant will need time to draw on sources of guidance before making suggestions. There may be some relevant research to be consulted, or possible models of good practice to visit and explore. Gradually it

175

becomes possible to develop a number of potential solutions. They should be *developed* as much as time will allow, that is, the detailed implications for staffing, resources, administration must be spelt out.

Third, when a final best solution is being proposed, the teachers involved need to be given time to assimilate the ideas before being asked to give their formal acceptance. They need time to make a mental evaluation of the proposed solutions, and opportunity to carry out simple, but private trials.

Fourth, it is wise to let the consultant keep contact with the teachers for some time after the period of cooperation is officially finished. Problems of implementation are bound to arise and teachers need to talk to someone about them. Fitting the new methods or new arrangements into the old may need a continuous 'after-sales' service. But gradually the teachers have to take over on a permanent basis.

If the improvement has been successful, there may be a feeling of 'we did it ourselves'. A good consultant would feel happy with this outcome, but consultants are also human beings, and a little credit and praise will usually be well-received!

Summary

1. There is a good case for a much wider use of outside help in the schools.
2. Advisory services, teachers' centres, local support services, local development projects, colleges and universities, major research projects, and the Schools Council represent the main sources of guidance and help.
3. Courses, resources, research, and consultancy are the main offerings available to schools.
4. Teachers need to develop more sophisticated approaches to the uses of outside consultants and helpers through:
   - knowledge acquisition;
   - building up relationships;
   - adopting systematic ways of cooperating with them.

14. Implementing a programme for the improvement of teaching

Two themes have dominated our discussion of the improvement of teaching:
1. Teaching is such a *complex* business that a systematic approach seems inevitable and necessary.
2. Teaching is such a *personal* matter that any attempts to improve it require great sensitivity on the part of all concerned.

It is often asserted that the 'systematic' approach and the 'humanistic' approach are opposites and mutually exclusive. This is like the debate in the industrial management field where 'scientific management' is contrasted sharply with the 'human relations' school of thought.

Somehow an integration of the two themes must be achieved. On the one hand, we cannot allow teaching to become a sort of mechanistic management system with tasks broken down into their tiny components and the procedures laid down with bureaucratic rigidity. Such a regime would be inimical to the very things which education is trying to promote. On the other hand, we cannot hope to run our classes on some idealized dream about the inherent goodness of man, his desire to achieve, and his ability to act in a responsible, creative, and knowledgeable way. Pupils at school are human, and they are young. They need the security and guidance which is offered to them in a well-structured and smoothly running system.

The real problem for the teacher is to recognize the value and importance of a *system*, while at the same time showing a proper concern for the *people* who will work within it. These two concerns must both be strong, but well-balanced, and mutually supportive.

The systematic approach

Our emphasis has been on a shift towards a more rational and deliberate approach to the planning, the preparation, and the teaching itself. This has led us to use the simple cycle described in the Introduction as a guide to activity. This proposed a thinking and planning phase, followed by an action phase, followed, in turn, by another thinking and planning phase, and so on.

We have shown in preceding chapters how such a systematic approach can be used in:

- course planning and preparation;
- general team management;
- the management of individual and small-group learning in the classroom;
- a programme for the improvement of teaching.

Figure 14.1 suggests a programme for course planning and team management. It is a two-year cycle. In September the team starts to review and evaluate its work during the last year. Later in the autumn term some ideas about the future begin to form, and the term enters a period of studies and investigation. This might include internal enquiries, systematic reading, attendance at courses, visits to other schools. The intention is to throw as much light as possible on the main areas of concern.

In the early part of the spring term the team identifies the 'key areas' for improvement for the forthcoming school year. Within these areas objectives will be formulated and the team will hope to name a difference. Later in the term the team is active in building up the support for its objectives, both within the team itself and externally. During the summer term, practical preparation takes over. Information is now available (or should be!) about staffing, finance, and administrative arrangements generally. The details of resources, timetabling, and schemes of work can be sorted out. When September comes the team should be ready to implement all the thinking, planning, and preparation of the last twelve months. Meanwhile, of course, another year has

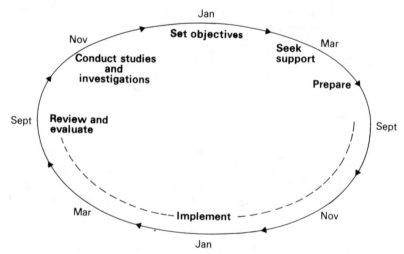

Fig. 14.1 *The planning and team management cycle*

gone by, and there is a year's work to be reviewed and evaluated. It is the sign of a well-managed team that it is *always* operating simultaneously in the present (teaching, marking, organizing, etc.) and in the future (planning and preparing).

Figure 7.1 (p. 93) suggested a cycle for the management of individual learning in the classroom. The length of the cycle could vary substantially according to the age and intellectual maturity of the pupil. The review and evaluation is carried out individually after the pupil's work in the last contract has been marked. This is followed by briefing, usually in a division or a small group. At the end of this a new individual contract is made and the study tour starts. Appropriate task cards are first collected and these guide the pupil towards the necessary resources, whether in the classroom or elsewhere. The work now progresses; tests are taken as appropriate, and the pupil completes the cycle by handing in work for marking and in anticipation of the next review. There are some satisfying aspects of this cycle in the eyes of the pupil—a sense of steady rhythm which provides a firm control of time; a sense of being left with a reasonable amount of time in which to organize oneself without interference; a sense of accountability which leads to a feeling of real responsibility.

Figure 14.2 represents the cycle for the improvement of classroom management which was described in Chapter 8. Forming and strengthening the team and devising a Policy for Teaching are the first essential tasks of this cycle. They need not be reviewed at the completion of each cycle and so they are shown on a loop. Review should not be left too long, however. Much of the benefit of a Policy for Teaching is for the debate it will generate each time that it is reviewed. The main cycle starts when the teacher evaluates his own teaching in the light of the Policy for Teaching. This is followed by a selection of key areas for improvement

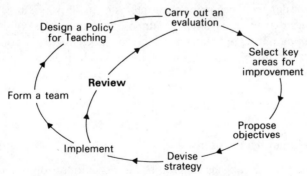

Fig. 14.2 *A cycle for the improvement of teaching*

and a more detailed statement of the specific improvement desired. Strategies are then devised and tried out in the classroom. A subsequent review is made in order to determine the extent to which the new strategies have been successful. The teacher following this cycle is in a much stronger position if working with a friendly colleague, who can act as confidant and observer.

The dangers of the systematic approach

Adopting a systematic approach is not necessarily a sure guarantee of instant success. There are likely to be failures on the way and some disappointments. A few practical suggestions may help to avoid some of these.

Look wide for support

It is difficult to adopt a systematic approach entirely on one's own. Our emphasis has been on the team approach. But it needs to go further than that. The sympathy and support of others is needed, particularly those who have control of finance and resources, and those who are influential in forming opinion. Cultivate a wide circle of supporters.

Give the programme a sustained effort

The danger is to try a programme of improvement and to give up at the first sign of difficulty. Mistakes are bound to be made, and some support may be lost. But persistence in this kind of activity really does pay off.

Avoid 'programmitis'

This is the danger of becoming more interested in the programme than in the things that the programme is supposed to serve. The symptoms of 'programmitis' are: too many meetings; too much documentation; rigid procedures; the exclusion of any activity which does not fit into the Programme. Common sense, flexibility, a sense of humour, and a realization that a programme will not automatically solve problems, will all help to keep things sane.

Beware 'behavioural objectives'

There is a well-established literature on 'behavioural objectives'. The high priests of this movement believe that objectives can and should be stated with complete precision and should be formulated after an intensive analysis of the 'behaviours' which the educator or manager wishes to promote. The test of a good objective is: can it be observed and measured? This is an extreme philosophy. It leads to the trivialization of objectives, and to very long lists. There is nothing wrong with using observable behaviour as an *indicator* of what ought to happen educationally; but it would be wrong to regard the behaviour as an obligatory way of defining it.

Aim high

Making improvements is hard work. It involves much planning and effort, a great deal of uncertainty, and a high risk of failure. It is often just as difficult to make a minor improvement as to achieve a major innovation. So it is worth being bold on occasions and going all out to make a real difference. A high proportion of the bold new ventures will result in 'failure', but only partially so, and it is worth remembering that the really significant advances are made by learning from these 'failures'. Oscar Wilde said it neatly: 'Experience is the name we give to our mistakes'. This is a profound truth in the improvement and innovation business. So go all out to make a real difference.

People and change

We have argued that systematic approaches will pay off. But improvements and innovation depend also on people. Creating the environment in which people can improve and innovate is a major concern for all professionals. It has got to be a mutually supportive exercise; it would be wrong to try to pin the responsibility on any individual or at any one level. What are the characteristics of such an environment in which improvement and change will flourish? How does it differ from an environment in which the emphasis is on stability and security?

Some characteristics of an environment which encourages improvement and change

1. Objectives are 'owned' by all the people and there is a constant generation of ideas.
2. Problems are shared and people are not too afraid to admit failures, or to seek help.
3. People support each other *personally* and are ready to deal with each other as whole people not merely as functionaries.

4. All opinions are respected and listened to; status or seniority are not used as excuses for patronizing behaviour.
5. Crises and conflicts are dealt with openly, cooperatively, and calmly.
6. Styles vary according to situations and needs.
7. Improvements and innovations are the prerogative of all and not confined to a few leaders.
8. Confidence and trust are evident throughout.
9. The structure of the organization approximates more to the organic system rather than the bureaucratic (see Chapter 4).

It is not easy to create this kind of world. It has to be built up patiently over a number of years, requiring the crises that test it, the successes that encourage it, and a wide range of experiences to enrich the thinking that supports it. It needs the commitment of a large number of people at all levels of status and seniority. The part that each can play will now be examined in some detail.

The importance of the Head

The Head who would aspire to run such an organization where improvements in the quality of the classroom is marked, must start with an examination of his own role and responsibilities in that direction. Within his own school there is a tendency for the Head to remain very powerful, in spite of a marked shift away from the autocratic image of the past. The Head tends to be the final judge as to what is right and what has to be done. This can so easily deteriorate into a permanent right of veto. It is easy to see that new ideas have dangers attached to them, have flaws in their reasoning, or may not be sufficiently well developed. The temptation to say no is always there; the easy reaction is to point out problems and possible difficulties, and to give an impression of wisdom and moderation. Unfortunately this has the effect of stifling initiative. It is better not only to encourage ideas, but also to be constantly asking the question, 'What can I do to convert this idea into something practical and useful?' This may mean giving a little time to the ideas which at first sight seem wild and impractical.

It is the Head's job actively to encourage the 'floating' of ideas, and this can only be done by reacting to them in a positive way. A positive and sympathetic reaction at first can often pave the way for serious reflective thought on the post of the teacher who presented the proposal. Modifications may well follow and there will have been much learning in the process.

Head teachers need to redirect their thinking back to the classroom.

There has been a marked tendency in recent years, especially in the secondary schools, for the Head of a school to be less and less concerned with the actual classroom work. Powerful forces are at work: more legislation; a desire for more involvement by councillors, governors, parents; more pressures from the unions; a trend towards more central control. The Head can be easily forgiven for adopting a role which is increasingly political and administrative, yet, at the same time, this must be seen as a neglect of the major aims of the school as an organization. We have only to consider other professions, looking at them from outside, to get a sense of perspective on this issue. Our greatest respect is surely for the consultant physician who has his own personal caseload, the senior barrister who personally takes the difficult cases, the professor who distinguishes himself in teaching or research.

These people also live and work in a political and administrative context, but regard it as a means to an end, not the end itself. And it is a poor and spiritless argument to claim that the new trend is towards an 'enabling' or 'facilitating' role. Teaching is too important and complex to be fobbed off with this. So what should the Head do?

First, he should arrange to teach, and arrange it carefully. This must not be a mere token gesture on the timetable in order to 'maintain credibility' since no one would be taken in by that. The teaching should be quite small in quantity (at least in the big secondary school), because we are not aiming to establish a record for stamina. It should be in the area (age group and subject) in which the Head feels personally most competent. It must be properly protected from routine interruptions. And then the Head must teach to the very best of his ability and also get involved in a programme for the improvement of teaching. The amount of teaching therefore *must* be small, in order to focus on quality. This is vastly preferable to the well-intentioned 'filling-in', often on a large scale, which merely has the effect of inducing tiredness and a sense of futility.

Second, he should redirect attention back to the quality of classroom work. Personal involvement will be a source of strength. But, in addition, there is a need to demonstrate the importance of 'a programme for the improvement of teaching', by *actively* giving support to those teachers who come forward with ideas, and who are ready to carry out experiments. Some kind of formal recognition of this work should be made.

Third, Heads need to reconsider how they might reward high quality classroom work. There is nothing to prevent promotion to higher scales being based entirely on the quality of a teacher's classroom work. In practice, there are so many other things that have to be done in the school as well that Heads feel obliged to tie them to promotions. But there is no reason why these extraneous activities should be accepted as the *only* reasons for promotion. There is no need to be explicit on this point, and the importance of the classroom needs to be asserted.

The importance of the team leader

The team leader occupies a key position in the improvement of teaching. Many of the responsibilities and tasks have already been described.

One important point remains. Most teachers are appointed to the role of team leader without having had any training or specific preparation for the job. There is a need for a thorough examination of education for middle management within the profession. A programme of education would rightly concern itself with general management issues such as curriculum planning, structures, and communications. But a major focus should be on systems for the improvement of teaching. Many team leaders working in schools today are acutely aware of their responsibilities in this matter, and are desperately seeking guidance. They need models of improvement strategies which will help them devise their own. Above all, they need help in the management of the human side of all this work. This would include such things as work organization, job design, human resource planning, selection, appraisal, staff development and training, motivation, leadership, participative management, discipline.

The job of team leader is a tough one and it has become a critical point in our education system. For example, in the secondary school the heads of department collectively probably have a bigger influence than the Head on the quality of education in the school. It is therefore all the more disturbing to realize the extent to which many team leaders are forced to work in comparative isolation. Their contacts with colleagues doing similar work and facing similar problems are generally inadequate. They have a need to spend time with each other exploring possible solutions to their problems, exchanging information and ideas, giving and receiving assistance.

The importance of consultants

This leads us naturally to all these people, local authority advisers, college and university personnel, teachers' centre wardens, staff of support and development agencies, who have a responsibility for helping teachers in their work.

It is a sad fact of life in our education system that on obtaining a job outside a school a teacher usually ceases to teach. Individuals are not entirely to blame; the system and the conventions simply do not help. But it is a weakness for our education service without doubt, and one can only speculate as to the damage that this unfortunate convention may have caused. It would be good if this trend could be reversed. As in the case of the Heads, any teaching undertaken by a consultant must not be a token gesture. It must be small in quantity, but high in quality, and undertaken openly as a natural and essential component of the consultant role. It should provide opportunity to gain new experience, to try out new ideas and materials, to serve as an exemplar not of 'perfect' teaching but of a systematic approach to improvement. From a 'base' like this the consultant will be in a strong position to contribute to a development programme of considerable potential. Such a programme would emphasize self-development, teacher participation, and it would be centred on the classroom. The consultant might feel able, from his own classroom experience, to advise directly on classroom matters. The consultant who can be practical about the details of classroom management is in a strong position because so frequently problems do need to have solutions worked out in detail. But to emphasize this too much would be to miss the real potential of consultancy. The 'expert' consultant role is 'telling' or 'giving' or 'showing'. Beyond this is the 'learning process' consultant who, by asking questions and providing conceptual frameworks, is helping in the process of learning. Beyond this again is the 'self-development' consultant who is giving a very personal kind of support to a teacher who is acquiring the ability to formulate the problems, seek the necessary support, and to generate his own scheme of self-renewal.

Consultancy can go very deep, but it needs confidence and the necessary skills appropriate to each level in order to be successful. We do not have a great deal of experience in consultancy of this kind and it is an area in which there is a need for systematic training.

The importance of the teacher

Ultimately any real improvement will depend on the individual teacher, and that is why self-development is so important. Whatever new problems are forced on to the schools in the future, the teacher will be the person who will have to cope. He will have to be strong enough and adaptable enough to match the improvements in his teaching to the changed world of tomorrow. Strength and adaptability can only come from cooperation, from disciplined thinking, and from a well-developed philosophy of improvement through self-renewal. That is the challenge.

Summary

1. The systematic approach relies on the concept of a cycle of improvement which can operate on many areas, over different time scales, and at different levels in the school.

2. The imperatives of the systematic approach are to look wide, to sustain effort; to avoid 'programmitis'; to beware of 'behaviour objectives'; to aim high.

3. The ideal environment for improvement has shared objectives and problems; mutual personal support; all opinions respected; crises and conflicts dealt with openly; improvements and innovations widespread confidence and trust; an 'organic' rather than 'bureaucratic' structure.

4. The Head's contribution:
   - personal example;
   - support for programmes of improvement;
   - rewards for high quality teaching.

5. The team leader's contribution. The vital need for training in general management, in systems for the improvement of teaching, in leadership functions.

6. The consultant's contribution:
   - the consultant as 'expert';
   - the consultant as 'learning process' helper;
   - the consultant as 'self-development' helper.

7. The teacher's contribution. Ultimately real improvements will depend on the teacher. The future will require strength and adaptability. The responses should be through cooperation, disciplined thinking, and a well-developed philosophy of improvement through self-renewal.

Bibliography and references

BARNES, D. (1975) *From Communication to Curriculum*, Penguin, Harmondsworth.

BARNES, D., BRITTON, J. and ROSEN, H. (1971) *Language, the Learner and the School*, Penguin, Harmondsworth.

BLOOM, B. (1971) *Handbook of Formative and Summative Evaluation*, McGraw-Hill, New York.

CLEGG, A. and MEGSON, B. (1968) *Children in Distress*, Penguin, Harmondsworth.

DAVIES, I. K. (1971) *The Management of Learning*, McGraw-Hill, London.

DAVIES, W. J. K. (1980) *Alternative to Teaching in Schools and Colleges*, Council for Educational Technology, London.

DENHAM, C. and LUBERMAN, A. (eds) (1980) *Time to Learn*, National Institute of Education, Washington.

D.E.S. (1977 and 1978) *Gifted Children in Middle and Comprehensive Secondary Schools*, HMI Series: Matters for Discussion 4, HMSO, London. *Mixed Ability Work in Comprehensive Schools*, HMI Series: Matters for Dicsussion 6, HMSO, London.

DUKE, D. L. (ed.) (1979) *Classroom Management*, The Seventy-eighth Yearbook of the National Society for the Study of Education, NSSE, Chicago.

DUNKIN, M. J. and BIDDLE, B. J. (1974) *The Study of Teaching*, Holt, Reinehart and Winston, New York.

DYAR, D. A. and GILES, W. J. (1974) *Improving Skills in Working with People*, Interaction Analysis, HMSO, London.

FLANDERS, N. (1970) *Analysing Teaching Behaviour*, Addison-Wesley, Reading, Massachusetts.

GAGE, N. L. (ed.) (1976) *The Psychology of Teaching Methods: Seventy-fifth Yearbook of the National Society for the Study of Education*, NSSE, Chicago.

GALTON, M. and SIMON, B. (1980) *Progress and Performance in the Primary School*, Routledge and Kegan Paul, London.

GALTON, M., SIMON, B. and CROLL, P. (1980) *Inside the Primary Classroom*, Routledge and Kegan Paul, London.

HANSON, J. (1975) *The Use of Resources*, Allen and Unwin, London.

HAVELOCK, R. G. (1973) *The Change Agent's Guide to Innovation in Education*, Educational Technology Publications, New Jersey.

187

BIBLIOGRAPHY AND REFERENCES

JOHN, D. (1980) *Leadership*, Heinemann Educational, London.

MARLAND, M. (1975) *Head of Department*, Heinemann Educational, London.

MARLAND, M. (1975) *The Craft of the Classroom*, Heinemann Educational, London.

ROMISZOWSKI, A. J. (1974) *The Selection and Use of Instructional Media*, Kegan Page, London.

ROMISZOWSKI, A. J. (1981) *Designing Instructional Systems*, Kegan Page, London.

SIMON, A. and BOYAR, E. G. (1970) *Mirrors for Behaviour*, Research for Better Schools, Philadelphia.

TABA, A. (1962) *Curriculum Development: Theory and Practice*, Harcourt, Brace and World, New York.

TAYLOR, L. C. (1972) *Resources for Learning*, Penguin, Harmondsworth.

THORNBURY, R., GILLESPIE, J. and WILKINSON, G. (1979) *Resource Organisation in Secondary Schools*, Council for Education Technology, London.

TOFFLER, ALVIN (1973) *Future Shock*, Pan, London.

WRAGG, E., GATES, J. and GUMP, P. (1976) *Classroom Interaction*, The Open University Press, Milton Keynes.

Index